Outside the Oven

Observations on life and business from
an entrepreneur and philosophical baker

Chris Duke

ISBN-10: 1973813254

ISBN-13: 978-1973813255

This book is dedicated to my wife Debbie and my daughter Anna. Without their love and support, none of this would have been possible.

Table of Contents

Forward

I've recently had an opportunity to reflect on experiences and what I've learned from decades of remarkable change in my personal and professional life. My professional career includes experience in the steel, heavy manufacturing, and energy industries along with federal, state, and local government agencies and dozens of technology and software businesses from concept through startup to growth stage. In the early 1990s I became a student of change having lived through rather tumultuous events during the past decade which gave me business insights and resilience that only this type of experience can provide. I'm thankful that I am blessed with family members and friends who exhibited abundant patience and supported me through my various career maneuvers.

My professional journey started with lengthy tours of duty in technology roles with two very large Fortune 500 public companies. In the mid-1980s, I discovered the DOD ARPANET as a means to interconnect disparate email systems and several years later I was totally mesmerized and energized by the incredible transformation that was emerging about private sector applications of the new Internet by smart entrepreneurs. During the mid-1990s I lobbied hard and was ultimately successful in landing my first role in a technology start-up business. After several decades working for large public companies I felt like I was in my early 20s again.

My entrepreneurial business opportunities allowed me to wear virtually every hat in an organization, from product management roles in pioneering technology organizations to sales, marketing, business development, operations, financial, and technology positions. I worked closely with tech companies in Silicon Valley and some of our finest scientists and engineers during a five-year consulting engagement with

NASA. I engaged with extraordinary executive talent through my executive recruiting business and with clients, partners, and colleagues in every continent. My journey also included the exhilaration of an IPO and the opportunity to launch several of my own services-based businesses.

Through all of this, I have enjoyed working with dozens of remarkable business professionals and entrepreneurs who have had a remarkable and lasting impact on me as a leader, manager, colleague, father, husband, sibling, and friend. Some of these key influencers had the patience and wisdom to teach me essential hard skills that were the foundation of positioning me to land new roles. Others have influenced me with critical soft skills based on how they have lived their lives both professionally and personally.

One of the overarching lessons that my life experience has taught me is that I judge character and performance from an individual's actions and the respective results, not just words. I've met far too many professionals who are extraordinarily successful in selling themselves and making grand promises, but often fall short on delivering results. I believe that actions and results are the essential gauge for judging an individual's integrity, what has become a critical factor in identifying the people that I want to invest my professional and social time.

Several of the fundamental lessons and guiding principles that I have learned through this journey include:

Treat people with **R**espect. That begins with your family members, employees and colleagues, customers, suppliers, and business partners. Lead with empathy, including a continuous focus on understanding your customer's specific needs and challenges and being creative to identify opportunities that add value to their lives and businesses. I believe it is also imperative to maintain a 360-degree perspective in your decision-making, searching for Win-Win-

Win (i.e. your customers, your business, and your suppliers) solutions. Live your life personally and professional with integrity by consistently following your own True North compass.

Maintain an unwavering, steadfast, and resolute focus on **Execution**. In my experience, this is truly the "Holy Grail" that separates world-class companies from all others. It is imperative that you empower those around you to achieve your goals, maintain a continuous process improvement, and leverage technology innovation that delivers a smart Return on Investment.

Instill a consistent level of **Accountability** across your organization with an emphasis to ensure that words and actions are consistently aligned. Accountability and integrity are vital in both our personal and professional lives.

Commit to continuous life-long **Learning**. This becomes ever increasingly more important every year of our lives as everything around us is changing at an ever-increasing pace and the world is truly getting smaller based on advances in digital and media technology platforms. Increasing access to information is a blessing and a curse today due to the overwhelming sources and access to all things digital. It is important to challenge ourselves to be proactive in filtering out valuable information from reliable sources across multiple disciplines.

These four **REAL** principles continue to guide my daily life, purpose, and actions.

Inside the Creative Mind and Authentic Heart of the Author of "Outside the Oven"

I met Chris Duke during 1999 at the crest of the "Dot Com Boom" and had the incredible fortune to have Chris join me on one of my most exhilarating roller coaster rides with a true ecommerce pioneering business during the Internet Boom period on the cusp on an IPO on NASDAQ. He was a trusted business partner at my side while we grew our team of restless pioneers from a handful to several dozen practically overnight. Chris led our supplier team and played a very strategic role in expanding our business into Europe. Occasionally the stars align and you have the distinct pleasure to work with individuals who possess remarkable skills and experiences that are synergistic to your own which ultimately positions your team to deliver amazing results beyond expectations.

Chris is an extraordinary serial entrepreneur who has demonstrated considerable perseverance and resilience throughout his life. He brings a unique balance of extraordinary tech savvy and smarts along with a very high degree of emotional intelligence. I continue to be astonished how Chris is able to bake 1,200 cookies in the morning, integrate two disparate cloud-based solutions in the afternoon, and rebuild a car engine in the evening. Chris has been an invaluable accountability partner for me personally since I launched my independent consulting practice a dozen years ago. I have thoroughly enjoyed our lengthy discussions and debates on his various entrepreneurial business ventures during this period including Google Hangouts Scheduler and Inside the Cloud to name just a couple.

I've published many of my personal and professional experiences and lessons learned over the past several decades in several books including 'The IT Leadership Pyramid', 'SMART Growth', and the 'Operational Proficiency Model'. Chris was instrumental as an adviser, editor, and graphics designer in the last two books.

Chris continues to inspire me with his ability to be incredibly resourceful in finding very creative and cost-effective tools, professional resources, and approaches to deliver solutions to his clients. This is another fundamental sign of a successful entrepreneur. One illustration is the success that Chris has enjoyed with the consistent placement of Anna's Gourmet Goodies in on-line search results, leading to many new clients nationwide without spending vast sums of advertising and sponsorship dollars. Of course, the virtually free word-of-mouth marketing based on the consistent delivery of high-quality products and services continues to be invaluable for his business.

Several years ago, I had the opportunity to spend several long days with Debbie and Chris as an apprentice at Anna's Gourmet Goodies in advance of the busy Christmas holiday season. While I should have not been at all surprised, I was extremely impressed at the process sophistication and level of automation in the raw materials and resource planning for baking cookies that ultimately follows methods created hundreds of years ago. This is coming from a guy that has spent several decades in process optimization using Six Sigma statistical methodologies. Chris has also mastered development of a very reliable supply chain of farmers and producers that consistently meet his extraordinary high-quality standards for his raw ingredients.

I would be remiss for not mentioning how much my family, friends, and business associates have thoroughly enjoyed Anna's gourmet cookies and brownies over the years. Unfortunately, I missed the SciQuest 'Cheesecake Bake-Off' and the genesis of Anna's Gourmet Goodies, but look forward to my Artisan Cookie treats on a frequent basis.

I must confess that I have learned a great deal through my interactions with Chris that have enriched my own personal guiding principles. He leads with a generous heart and a consistent True North guiding compass and has taught me much about Paying it Forward through his charitable and professional networking actions over the past two decades.

Chris is a gifted storyteller and I continue to look forward to reading each 'Outside the Oven' blog post and calling him afterward to discuss the story behind each story with him personally.

Jack Spain
President, Spain Business Advisors

Introduction

I've always been interested in the back story. Whether it's someone I meet, a place I visit or a product I use, I find the details that surround the person, place or thing create the richest memories. There's a side of me that loves math, numbers, statistics and data, but the other part of me loves a great story.

When I look back at my childhood and early years I have memories of stories that are thick as honey. Long before the Internet and Social Media were even a concept, I grew up with parents, aunts, uncles, friends and neighbors who all shared stories not just from their life and their work, but from their experiences. I learned a lot about life listening to their stories.

Fast forward to 1999 and I was working at SciQuest, once a dotcom darling during the IPO frenzy when money flowed like water over Niagara Falls. The pace of work and change exceeded anything I've ever experienced. It was exciting, even though it sometimes felt like being inside a pinball machine.

The experiences I had there were invaluable. Seven job descriptions or titles in four years meant that I was continually learning something new. I traveled to Western Europe and learned about business and culture from a different perspective, picking up stories along the way. I drank the Kool-Aid and it tasted sweet.

But then, things began to unravel. The realities of expenses that far exceed income set in. Management changed. Culture shifted. Layoff announcements were a regular event as the number of people in the office continued to shrink and the company struggled to find its identity in the market. The founders had a great story, but in this case, it was simply not enough.

Sometime late in 2000, my wife Debbie and I began to think about our life and what we might want to do. SciQuest provided a good lifestyle, but the hours were long and Anna's toddler years were slipping by quickly. I had not run my own business since the last one crashed and burned in 1993. But I felt the tug.

When SciQuest still had money in the bank, we put on fun events that were the hallmark of the dotcom days. One of those was a 'Cheesecake Bake-Off'. I hadn't really planned on entering, but the night before I decided to cobble together a recipe and give it a try. My Mom used to bake a cheesecake that included a topping of sour cream added after the initial cheesecake was finished. After she died, I was able to copy her recipe box that included instructions on how to make this cheesecake. It was on a well stained card with the name 'Ms. Fischer' listed as the source. The card and the box are a whole other story.

I tweaked it a bit, adding a graham cracker and date crust, some apples sautéed in Bourbon and a caramel drizzle on top. I'm sure neither Mom nor Ms. Fischer ever thought of this concoction, but it worked well enough that I was crowned 'Grand Champion'. I remember that day vividly and in some ways, it was the start of this leg of my journey.

It took a little while, but eventually Debbie and I incorporated a company that is now known as Anna's Gourmet Goodies, Inc. We had a very short stint in some other areas of business, but after getting all the necessary licenses, inspections and insurance settled on building a business around baking and selling wholesale desserts for restaurants. For years, my Mom told me the story of my grandmother baking pies with fruit from their farm and selling them to a local restaurant to help support their family of nine children. Starting this business was simply a matter of that story coming full circle.

We continued to grow the business part time while I was working at SciQuest. We added customers and equipment as the business took on a life of its own. In 2002, we expanded our facilities and built a new commercial bakery. Having started businesses in the past and watching the slow death of the dotcom business boom, we practiced responsible financial management which included sweat equity, shopping auctions and warehouses for equipment and learning to manage our resources frugally.

By 2003, we had a customer base that ordered from us on a regular basis, a website up and running, a completely furnished and debt free bakery operation and a little financial cushion in the bank. After much thought, planning and prayer, I decided to take a leap of faith and leave SciQuest. Like most stories, you can't really see how they play out until after the fact. In retrospect, it was the right time for me to go.

We grew the business to be about as large as our equipment and freezer capacity would allow. It was at that point we had a stark realization - it was not enough. Being in the wholesale business means that you survive on volume. If you can't produce enough volume, you won't survive. We thought about expanding and growing this part of the business, but a small seed we planted was beginning to take root.

We had shipped some of our frozen desserts to customers via the website. It was painfully expensive, but the idea of creating a personalized experience with customers was appealing. And while I'm certain that the restaurants who served our desserts were getting their fair share of customer complements, Anna's Gourmet Goodies didn't really get to participate in the story.

I talked with friends in various industries and decided to put together gift boxes of cookies. They didn't require refrigeration, were much easier to ship and we could package them in a way that would create an experience for the recipient. Baking and shipping cookies or other food gifts via the Internet was not a new idea. We sampled and studied the competition to see what worked for us, and what did not.

We kept the wholesale side of the business going as that was generating cash while we figured out how to grow the cookie gift business. Like any business, we tried different paths to find customers. We conducted demos for Realtors, participated in trade shows, sampled cookies and the like. Some things worked and some did not. During that time one thing became clear - people seemed to light up when I told the story of our business.

I was probably a little late getting into the blogging game. I had a false start in 2006, but finally launched OutsideTheOven.com in 2008 to share stories not just about our business, but the back stories of life as an entrepreneur baking cookies, raising a family and building a business. I wrote and posted to the blog. There was an occasional comment, but for the most part I was never sure if anyone was really reading. Still, it felt like the right thing to do for our business.

It wasn't until I met Chris Brogan and received a loving but firm whack on the side of the head, that I changed how I share the stories. I was referred to Chris by Phil Buckley, a friend and SEO expert who said I might want to follow him. I signed up for his newsletter at ChrisBrogan.com and took one of his online courses. The first 'whack' came when I sent him a copy of one of my email newsletters. I can't remember exactly how he phrased it, but it was something like a 'keyword stuffed jumble of marketing jargon'. Not exactly the response I was hoping for, but one that I certainly needed.

I stepped back a bit and thought about our story and how we connect with customers. Instead of sending out emails filled with coupons, offers, new products and the like, maybe I should simply start sharing my stories posted on OutsideTheOven.com. I did just that.

I first realized the power of stories at a trade show put on by the Raleigh Chamber of Commerce. A man who was walking down the aisle stopped by our booth. I didn't recognize his name as a customer or even someone I had met, and I'm pretty good at remembering a face. He said, 'I love reading your stories I get in my email.' It was the first time I realized that there were indeed people out there, other than a close relative, who actually read the stories and were positively impacted.

Since that time I've received more than a few email replies and comments from others on our email list about how a particular story touched them in some way. One of the most moving came from my friend Antony who replied to the story about the US Post Office helping us stop delivery of a package to a customer whose wife had recently died. Antony's wife had recently passed from ALS and it really struck a chord with him because of the number of letters and packages still arriving for his wife.

I've not followed the rules of other bloggers in terms of frequency of articles. Stories come when they come. Has it made an impact on our business? I believe it has based on the feedback we get from our customers. That's certainly a goal of writing the blog, but not the only one. I have readers who are not customers who have told me they are inspired by what they read. If just one reader makes a connection between my experience and their work or business, that checks a box for me.

Drew Bridges, a local author and former bookstore owner once told me that "Writers write not because they want to, but because they have to." I can say with certainty that sharing stories on OutsideTheOven.com is not easy for me. But it is something I feel compelled to do. Not just because it is good for business, but out of a desire to connect with readers at an emotional level and inspire them to step back, contemplate their journey, and get outside the oven.

Identity

"A great business has to have a conscience. You have to know who you are and who you are not. "

-Howard Schultz

The rest of the story

Original Post Date: October 1, 2012

I'm a radio fan and for me, one of the greatest story tellers of all time is Paul Harvey. I shared this post both as a tribute to my aunt after her passing, and to reveal the origin of our company name beyond simply naming it after my daughter. Everyone has a story, including you. Every company has a story, including yours or the one you work for. Before the written word existed, humans communicated via stories. Now that we are bombarded with more written words than are possible for anyone to digest, the power of a story is greater than ever before. This is a part of our 'back story', what's yours?

I've probably told the story of Anna's Gourmet Goodies and how it all started maybe a thousand times or more. From casual conversations to small groups to classes filled with MBA students, I've shared the ups and downs, the ins and outs of starting this business. But there is a piece of the story that I've never talked about, until now.

This picture features my daughter Anna (the primary business namesake) and my mother's sister, Lois Bradley. Aunt Lois (as almost everyone I know calls her) is the one Aunt from my mother's family that I'd have to say I have spent the most time with, all my life. From my earliest memories of childhood throughout my adult life, there are pages and chapters filled with memories that belong to Aunt Lois.

My mother, Anna Duke, was one of nine children and most of her brothers and sisters lived not too far from Louisville, Kentucky where I grew up. I don't recall exactly how often we got together to have dinner, but it was frequent enough for me to develop two very strong memories; family and food. Whether it was simply going to Aunt Lois' house for Sunday dinner, or a holiday gathering at our house, it seemed that getting together with my Aunts, Uncles and cousins was a common event. And there was always plenty of food and desserts on the table.

I can remember a number of occasions where Mom would take me over to Aunt Lois' grand old house on Village Drive in Louisville. I remember that place almost as if I lived there. The cracks in the steps. The time weathered brick exterior. The fragrant, yet musty smell of an old house. And the kitchen.

On one occasion when I was probably about five years old, Mom dropped me off to spend the night sometime around the Christmas holidays. I walked into the kitchen where Aunt Lois was busy working and announced with a big smile, "I've got a surprise for you!" "Well, what is it Christopher Robin" she said. "We're going to make some cookies!" I announced.

Aunt Lois laughed and you guessed it, we made cookies. Was that the tiny mustard seed that lay dormant for so many years before it turned into my work? Perhaps.

As it is with most families, the road of life is rarely straight and almost never a four-lane highway. Aunt Lois moved to Maryland and opened a business with my Uncle Brad. I went to college then moved to North Carolina.

In the late 80's, I found myself in a particularly stormy time in life. Mom had died, my first business failed, and I landed back in Kentucky. Without a regular job or much money in the bank, I found a room and a bed at Aunt Lois' house in Frankfurt. Her husband, Uncle Brad, died some years ago, and she was, not surprisingly, willing to take on a roommate.

The house had changed, but the feeling of being around Aunt Lois was still the same as when I stood in her kitchen almost 25 years earlier. It was both a difficult time for me in some ways, but magical in others. We planted a garden. We went on trips. And we managed to cook up some goodies every now and then.

I don't remember exactly when I first heard Aunt Lois use the word, 'goodie'. It's one of those words you learn that you always associate with someone. I can remember her tasting something, most often a cookie or dessert, smiling and saying, "Boy, that's a goodie".

Add another 15 years to the calendar, and I find myself in North Carolina. I was working full time, but Debbie and I were starting a business, out of our home. I had this idea that I wanted to make really great desserts (later, that turned into the current cookie business). We thought about a name. I had a silhouette of Anna we had made at the North Carolina State Fair on my wall. Why not name it after her? But what else?

We came up with a number of different ideas, but I kept coming back to this word, goodie that had become a part of my vocabulary. How about 'Anna's Gourmet Goodies'? We mocked up the logo. Debbie agreed, and well, here we are.

Just like any good recipe, ingredients come together to make something greater than the individual parts. As it goes with most of our lives, we don't always see how these things will eventually came together, but I know that among the ingredients that make up Anna's Gourmet Goodies, Aunt Lois most certainly played a role.

On Saturday afternoon, September 29th at precisely 3:00 p.m., Lois Bradley took her last breath and exited this earth leaving behind a life well lived. Her son and two daughters were there to see her off. I don't know what your faith background tells you, but I'm absolutely certain that she was greeted warmly by, among others, her late husband, Colonel O.C. Bradley and my mother, the late Anna B. Duke. There is no doubt in my mind that God picked up a goodie on Saturday.

Born in 1921, Lois Bradley grew up one of nine children on a farm in Morehead, KY. She served in Women's Auxiliary Army Corp in WWII. She raised her family. Working at an electronics company in Louisville, she gave a now famous young woman her first job, Diane Sawyer. She and her husband started a high end glass and gift business. She was cast as Hiawatha's mother in a small independent film. And not too many years ago, she hung out with Gordon Lightfoot backstage after one of his concerts. Aunt Lois lived a rich, full and wonderful life.

It is never easy to say goodbye to a loved one who has, in so many subtle ways, had a profound impact on your life. But for me, the memories she leaves behind, are as rich and creamy as a double scoop of ice cream from our friends at Homeland Creamery.

On Wednesday, I'll help carry her remains to her final resting place in the Lexington Cemetery. After words of hope and faith, we'll hear the crack of rifles firing off a 21-gun salute. A solemn bugler will play taps.

Thank you, Aunt Lois, for all the things you did for me throughout my life. And whether I'm baking one, or a thousand cookies, I'll smile and remember that the roots of that love of making something really good trace back, in part, to your kitchen on Village Drive. I hope that everyone who has the opportunity to bite into a cookie from Anna's Gourmet Goodies will smile and say, "Boy, that's a goodie!"

Really outside the oven

Original Post Date: August 21, 2008

This was my first post to OutsideTheOven.com. When I'm asked the question, "Why did you start Anna's Gourmet Goodies?" the answer always revolves around the same topic - Anna. While it is entirely possible to work at a company or job and spend time with your child (or children), I knew that for me, I wanted more. I wanted both the time and the mental energy to be there for all the most important moments, and to create a few lasting ones as well. This was definitely one of those lasting moments.

Earlier this summer, Anna and I decided to get outside and float down the Neuse River. We had the opportunity to test drive a kayak on Falls Lake during a festival earlier in the spring and a trip down the river seemed like a fun way to spend a Saturday together. It was a great afternoon, even considering the surprise appearance by a slithering guest.

We headed out to Paddle Creek Outfitters located just off Falls of the Neuse Road in Raleigh. They set us up with a tandem kayak, paddles, and life jackets. Debbie helped prepare a cooler with some lunch and, of course, packages of our gourmet cookies for this 4-hour tour. We loaded the kayak on top of our Honda Element and headed down to the entry point.

It was a perfect day on the water. Not yet sweltering heat, but warm enough to make you feel good about being outside. Anna quickly learned how to use the paddles and we drifted slowly away from the dock, waving and looking forward to a nice afternoon together. We drifted for a couple of hours and then decided it might be time for a little lunch. I spotted what looked to be an abandoned picnic shelter just off the river and pulled the kayak onto the sand bar nearby. Having spent much of my youth around lakes and woods, I decided to hike up the bank and scout out the terrain first, just to make sure it was safe.

I walked cautiously through the weeds to the picnic area. It was a bit dusty, but it was shady and seemed like it might make a nice place to rest and enjoy the lunch Debbie packed for us. As I turned to go back down to get Anna, I looked down at the path just before stepping on a snake that had made its way into the narrow clearing. I was close enough to get as good a look as I cared for at the time and am pretty certain it was a water moccasin, heading back down for a swim.

The snake was directly between me and Anna. The cell phone was in the boat. Fathers are not supposed to panic – right? I yelled at Anna and told her not to move from the shore while I looked for something to encourage this local resident to move along. I found a stick that was way too short and a chunk of wood. I eased into position behind the snake and carefully tossed the chunk of wood just to the right of the snake, hoping he would opt for an exit, stage left, and not force me to use the stick. As luck would have it he complied and I sprinted down to the boat quick enough to make an Olympic coach proud.

Anna and I agreed that lunch in the boat seemed like a good idea, so we quickly hopped in and shoved off back into the water. The 'Master Dad' avoided an incident and managed to use this experience to offer up a few lessons for Anna – don't panic (or at least don't let anyone know), stay calm, and watch what is going on around you.

Anna's Gourmet Goodies affords us the luxury of having my daughter around most of the day while we work – thanks to our wonderful customers. It has truly been a blessing to be able to watch her grow up. But finding time to talk does not come easy when you run a business. There's always something to do, emails to answer, phone calls to return, website updates, or whatever. Being out on the water, in the boat, was just about the perfect way to spend time talking, listening, and re-connecting. It was a reminder just how important it is for us to 'disconnect' from the frantic pace of our everyday life and spend a little time outdoors with the folks who matter the most.

Hopefully you have found time to get outside your 'work zone' this summer. If you haven't, there's still time before we get too busy with school, holidays and work. I highly recommend kayaking, just watch where you step should you venture off into the weeds.

Being helpful got us started and keeps us going

Original Post Date: October 19, 2011

"How can I help?" If you strip away everything from a business, the name, location, products, and services - everything, at the core, a business must be of some help to survive. Business exists to help customers in some way. The degree to which a business does this and communicates their mission to the people who work there varies widely. The idea of being helpful to customers is something that is baked into the core of our business in no small part because that is how I grew up. Whether it was our church, another family member, or a neighbor, I learned very early in life that helping others is fundamental to our purpose here on earth.

When I have the opportunity to speak about starting a company, I take time to look back at where I've been, think about what I've learned along the way and try to pass on some of my best pearls of wisdom. I spoke during Career Day at Anna's school recently on what it's like to start a business and while I'm not clear on whether I inspired any of the students to become entrepreneurs, I did accomplish one of my goals of not embarrassing Anna and permanently injuring her social status with any of my stories.

When I look back at our journey starting Anna's Gourmet Goodies, I am struck by the number of people that have stopped to help me along the way. One of my managers early in my sales career, Don Brown, used to say that the nine most powerful words in the English language are, "I have a problem, and I need your help". It might seem like an overstatement, but the number of people that have said 'Yes, I can help', far outnumber those who've turned away.

A few months ago, the Kroger store in Wakefield Commons shopping center closed their doors. Some employees transferred to other company stores, while others found work at new businesses. Faye, one of the ladies in the bakery, went to work for a dry cleaner. She was one of the first people I remember helping me when we started Anna's Gourmet Goodies nearly ten years ago.

I wondered into the bakery one day and had some questions about packaging and where they purchased various items. Faye always had time to help and even sold us some supplies to get us started. I visited the store many times over the years and she always had a smile and a word of encouragement.

We started our business using flour from Lindley Mills. We found it in Whole Foods market where Mike Davis worked in the bulk food section. I knew a little about flour, but Mike was always very helpful whenever I had a question about anything in his area. We started buying in small quantities, but as our business grew, he helped us increase our capacity and reduce cost by ordering in bulk when we were too small to buy direct, but needed more than just a few pounds.

Our company grew by having people and business partners that were willing to help us with their time and expertise. I've always been grateful for that help and have incorporated that into our business model at Anna's Gourmet Goodies. Here are some areas where we actively practice being helpful for our customers:

- **Website.** I designed our website to be a friendly place with helpful information. When a customer comes to AnnasGourmetGoodies.com, we want them to be able to find the products and information they need – not just what we are trying to sell that day. A great website should be helpful to visitors.

- **Orders.** Before we ship an order, we import the address information and check it for validity. If it does not show up as a valid address, we'll first try to find the correct one if it is a small typo, then we'll contact the customer for clarification And if we find a typo in the message, we'll fix that as well. We help our customers by getting the gift to the right address with the right message.

- **History.** When a customer sets up a custom label or note card, we save that for later use. If a customer sends us a list, we save that as well in case there are questions in the future, or that want to use it again. We help by remembering the order details for our customers.

At Anna's Gourmet Goodies, we've adjusted our business with new products and ideas over the years, but a core principle of our company has not changed – we genuinely try to help people, whether or not they are a customer. We seek out and nurture those suppliers, business partners, and people that offer up their help and advice. By doing so, our goal is to build a community of loyal customers and suppliers who value what we do and share that experience with others who have similar beliefs.

We absolutely make outstanding gourmet cookies, but our passion for service and being helpful by offering our knowledge and expertise are key ingredients in all of our recipes.

Cookies and brownies baked with a bit of history

Original Post Date: November 4, 2014

The idea behind any business comes down to taking ingredients, combining them and creating something that is greater than the sum of the parts. Whether it is a product or service, survival depends on generating value that goes beyond the sum of the individual parts. In the baking business, most of the ingredients are familiar to virtually everyone and are probably in your pantry right now. So what makes the difference? The process of combining them or the recipe, matters. But I also learned that it is not just the quality of the ingredients that matters, but the quality of the business creating those ingredients can make a huge difference as well. We spend time choosing our suppliers for a reason.

Every business has a story and history, some longer than others. The supplier for our primary ingredient at Anna's Gourmet Goodies, organic whole wheat pastry flour, comes from a mill that was a business before America was a country. Founded in 1755 by Thomas Lindley, Lindley Mills operates at the same location and is run by a ninth generation descendant, Joe Lindley.

It's the only flour we've ever used for our cookies and brownies. And while I could get a distributor to deliver the product, I've made it a point to take time to get to know the folks at Lindley Mills and pick up our order at the mill. We usually stop in with a supply of our cookies made from their flour that are always well received. It might seem like a small thing, but I believe that having a personal connection to an ingredient produced by a descendant of the founder of a business started more than 254 years ago, adds more to our product than simply great flour.

The mill was the site of one of the largest and most hard fought engagements in North Carolina between the British Loyalists and the Whigs. Anna and I toured the battle ground some years ago where the markers tell the story.

On September 12, 1781, Loyalist leader David Fanning crept into the state capital, then in Hillsborough, secured the town and captured over 200 prisoners including Governor Thomas Burke. They moved the prisoners down to where the Wilmington road crossed Cane Creek at Lindley's Mill.

On the morning of September 13, the Whigs ambushed the Loyalists as they were crossing the branch, killing their commander, Colonel Hector McNeil. The Loyalists managed to secure the prisoners at the rear of the Spring Friends Meeting House and Fanning organized a flanking attack on the Whigs. The Whigs held their position for several hours, but were eventually driven back. Fanning, who was wounded, turned over command to Colonel McDugald who managed to reach Wilmington safely with the prisoners.

In total, more than 250 men on both sides were killed or wounded. They were cared for or buried by the local Quaker community. While not a victory for the Whigs, the battle served as a turning point, inspiring them to double their efforts, fight on to suppress the Loyalists and ultimately, win the war.

The mill was operated by the Lindley family for more than 100 years. After that, it changed hands and operated as a variety of grain related businesses. In 1975, two hundred and twenty years after opening, Thomas Lindley's descendants re-purchased and restored the mill to operation. They've been grinding organically grown grain there on the same site, for the past 39 years.

There are a lot of reasons why the cookies and brownies at Anna's Gourmet Goodies taste so good. We developed the recipes and the process we use to make each small batch, by hand. Rather than simply tell you 'we use the finest ingredients' (a phrase you'll find on just about every cookie or food site in the world) I thought you might like to know a little more about the history behind our ingredients.

We just picked up a large load of flour to begin getting ready for the holiday baking season. I placed our order with June and Dewey helped pull the bags. Mr. Joe was busy that day (as he usually is), but I'm pretty sure he managed to get one of the cookies we delivered. They loaded us up, and I stopped on my way out to snap this picture of the mill, surrounded by the brilliant colors of fall.

The history of Anna's Gourmet Goodies is relatively short, going back a scant few years to 2001 when Debbie and I founded the company after I won Grand Champion at the Cheesecake Bake-off Competition for my Apple-Bourbon Cheesecake (yes – that's another story). Lindley Mills not only provides us with a reliable source of a superior quality product, but adds an important ingredient to the soul of our business – a real sense of history and some perspective on time.

I always look forward to taking a ride out in the country to visit our friends at Lindley Mills whenever we need a load of flour and a dose of perspective. We'll carry it back to the bakery, mix it up with our other ingredients, and continue to turn out incredible cookies and brownies that are filled with passion, love and more than a little bit of history.

How this Jesuit Brother and baker influenced our business

Original Post Date: November 4, 2014

Hindsight is a term that often is associated with negative things, but I've found that it can be a good thing when used in the proper context. One of my favorite uses of this term is to look back at all the people who have shown up in my life at precisely the right moment to inspire me, move me forward, and help me change direction or otherwise guide me along a path. While we might never be able to perfectly see the ultimate impact of people we meet until long after the fact, it can serve as a guide for being more aware of who we meet in our daily life and how they may play a role in our journey. You never know how the next person you meet may impact your life and business.

One of the interesting things about starting a new business is that no matter what road you start down, there will always be twists and turns that take you in directions you could never have predicted. For Anna's Gourmet Goodies, one of those turns started out in Celebration, Florida at the National Pie Championships and carried us to the National Theater Workshop for the Handicapped in SoHo, Manhattan. That meeting and conversation with Brother Rick Curry, S.J. had a lasting impact on the business and my life.

In 2003, we joined the American Pie Council and planned our trip to the National Pie Competition in Celebration, Florida. We settled on three entries, Pumpkin Cream with Grand Marnier, Chocolate Kahlua Cream, and Real Key Lime. All made with our signature graham cracker and whole wheat pastry crust in a fluted pan.

Our story, combined with original and unique recipes were sure to secure an award and a spot in the pie maker history books. But alas, despite our best efforts, we left without a single prize. We managed to get a very brief appearance in the Food Network's coverage of the event, but that was the extent of our fame for the weekend.

On the ride home, Debbie was thumbing through a copy of Oprah magazine and came across an article about a bakery run by a Jesuit brother. He used the proceeds to fund the National Theater Workshop for the Handicapped. It was a great story. A Jesuit Brother, actor, author and master baker, pursing his passion, refusing to give up and helping others in a similar situation pursue their dreams. The challenges of running a non-profit and a business did not stop Rick Curry, despite the fact that he was born with only one arm.

I decided to reach out to Brother Curry and ask if he would meet with me. I had a business trip planned to NYC in the coming weeks and it seemed like the perfect opportunity. Thankfully, he agreed.

There are some people you meet in life where you feel an instant connection. Like being wrapped in a warm blanket with a cup of hot cocoa next to a crackling fire. That's what it felt like sitting down with Brother Curry. We exchanged stories about our lives growing up. He told me how he ended up where he was, doing the work he was doing. Through all the twists and turns, it was clear that he was on the right path.

We talked about Anna's Gourmet Goodies and the struggles of starting a business while working a job. Of trying to discern what I should do, and why. I shared what was then our tagline, "Our most important ingredient is love". He paused for a moment, and with a little mist starting to appear in his eyes and said, *"Chris, hold on to that. Don't ever lose it."*

Brother Curry was generous with his time that day. After laughing and exchanging more stories about life and baking, it was time for me to go. He picked up a copy of his book, **The Secrets of Jesuit Breadmaking** and signed it for me, *"To Chris, someone who will make a big difference through baking."* He gave me a big hug and I was on my way back to North Carolina with more to think about and another signpost to add to my collection on this journey.

Since then, I've referred to Brother Curry's book on many occasions. I'm particularly fond of the Challah and Brother Bandera's Italian bread, something I've made almost every Christmas for the past several years.

I made a few adjustments to Sister Courtney's Buttermilk bread and it came out fabulous

This weekend, Anna and I picked out a new recipe from the book, Sister Courtney's Buttermilk Bread. I modified it a bit, substituting olive oil for the shortening and baking rounds instead of loaves. It was wonderful. Light, soft, perfect with olive oil and homemade lasagna.

Despite my best intentions I have not connected with Brother Curry since that chance meeting, but I've never forgotten his wisdom and strive to focus on what matters most at Anna's Gourmet Goodies. I've looked him up a time or two online, but just never made it happen. I did another search and found that sadly, I missed the opportunity. He passed away on December 21, 2015 from heart failure.

It was a brief meeting, but an important milestone in our business and my life's journey. It's rare to meet someone with a heart and a smile as big as Brother Curry. I'm still in awe of how much he accomplished and I have kept my promise not to let go of our original ingredient list.

And if by chance Brother Curry is looking down on me from his Heavenly home I'd like to say thanks again for helping me along the way. You were definitely an important stop on the road worth traveling.

Afghanistan is now closer to home

Original Post Date: April 27, 2010

After more than seven years, it is still hard for me to share this story without getting a little choked up. I did not serve in the military but have a profound sense of gratitude for the men and women who made the decision to serve our country, sometimes putting themselves in harm's way, and sometimes giving the ultimate sacrifice. When you ask, they'll often say something like, "I'm happy to, just doing my job". In this case, I experienced some of that gratitude coming back to me for simply doing my job, baking and shipping cookies.

The postman delivered a priority mail box the other day. We receive a lot of shipments, but weren't really expecting anything in this type of box. I recognized the name as one of our customers from the military. We sent his unit some of our gourmet cookies a few years ago and he wrote me one of the most moving thank you letters I have ever received.

I opened the box, and the first thing that came out was a United States Flag, folded in military fashion in the shape of a triangle. My heart stopped beating for what seemed like a minute. I'm used to seeing flags like this when someone has been killed in action. Did something happen to one of the soldiers under his command? To our customer?

Inside there was a folder, and in it a certificate and a letter, addressed to Anna's Gourmet Goodies. The flag was presented to us as a thank you for support of the troops and the War on Terror and was actually flown over Bagram Airfield in Afghanistan. I felt a lump in my throat and my eyes swelled with tears of pride.

If you've been to our website lately, you might have noticed the tag line, "Our cookies make people happy". I've actually been using that for a few years now, after some deep thought as to what it is that we really do at Anna's Gourmet Goodies. It might seem obvious that we bake cookies, but I believe that great businesses have something that goes beyond the simple transaction of supplying goods and services. You might call it a soul.

From the very beginning, I have always poured my heart and soul into everything we do. Every product – every cookie, painstakingly measured by hand. Whether we are shipping an order for a Fortune 100 company, a wedding or event, the local realtor or mortgage broker, or to a group of men and women that put their lives at risk in places most of us would never consider going, we do it the same every time.

I can't help but think that those men and women who choose to serve our country in the armed forces are driven by a similar passion. They too, put their heart and soul into what they do. But unlike what we do at Anna's Gourmet Goodies, baking cookies, they put their lives at risk, sometimes paying a price far greater than my aching feet or tired hands. And they do it over, and over again. To be of service to these folks is indeed an honor and a privilege.

A few years ago, Rick Warren's book the 'Purpose Driven Life' spawned a new emphasis on the question human beings have been asking for thousands of years, "What is my purpose here on Earth?" Having read the book and taught a couple of classes on the subject, I've spent my share of time thinking about this very thing. I am fortunate enough to have had the opportunity to pursue many of my passions and to sometimes get a glimpse of what that purpose might be. Being of service to others and making people happy are certainly on the list.

After receiving the package, I downloaded and installed Google Earth. If you have not tried this application, I absolutely recommend you give it a drive. I measured a line from Wake Forest, NC to Bagram Air Base in Afghanistan and I come up with about 7,466 miles, more or less, as the crow flies. It's a long way no matter how you measure it, but it is certainly a place that is closer to me now, than ever before. I am connected in a way that Google Earth, the Internet, email, social media, or any of these electronic pathways cannot match. Because I know that in this far off land where I may never set foot, a group of young men and women opened up a package, took a bite out of a cookie that we mixed, baked and packaged by hand, and for at least that moment, were happy. For Anna's Gourmet Goodies, I'd have to say our mission was accomplished.

Sending a gift? We've got your back

Original Post Date: May 5, 2013

Keith Ferazzi's book really struck a chord with me because it hits on a concept that is a core element of our business and my personal life - trust. It's something that can take a long time to build, but can disappear in an instant. We are at a point and time in history when starting a business has never been easier, and trust has never been more vital. And as some of the largest businesses on the planet have discovered, even the smallest failure in trust can have devastating consequences. Mistakes will always happen, but in the end, it is the core intent and values of the business that matter.

When you're a customer at Anna's Gourmet Goodies, you can relax. We've got your back.

If you place an order at AnnasGourmetGoodies.com, you expect your gourmet cookie gifts to be baked fresh and sent to the recipient. You expect a card with your message to be in the box. You expect we'll send the right box, basket, or ribbon color. Whether it is a personal gift, or a corporate gift, you expect your order to be completed as placed. We've spent more than ten years shipping hundreds of thousands of cookies throughout the United States and Military bases around the globe, doing exactly that – fulfilling orders for our customers as expected. We're not perfect by any means, but we own up to any mistakes and always do the right thing for our customers.

Getting your order out the door correctly is important for everyone, but especially important for our business customers. Why? Corporate gifts are often sent to either clients or prospects. The last thing a business customer wants (or us for that matter) is for someone to receive a personalized business gift that misses the mark. While we can't guarantee everyone will love our cookies and brownies (yes – it is true that some people don't rave about our cookies), we go the extra mile and pay attention to the details we can control to deliver a memorable gift experience.

Here are just a few things we do for our business clients:

- **Typos in the message**. While there are times when typos are intentional, we always have a second look at the message on the order. If it is obvious this was due to fast fingers or a rouge smartphone, we'll fix it before it goes out. In some cases, if the wording doesn't sound right, we'll send an email to our customer to make sure everything is just right. We don't want to change the message or the intent, but if we catch those minor errors that might otherwise spoil the ideal gift, we both look better.

- **Address errors**. It happens. Maybe your customer relationship software is out of date, or there is a small typo. We load our orders into a database that checks addresses against the USPS database. If it does not come back with a 9-digit zip code, we'll first do some research on the Internet. Sometimes we can fix the error. If we still can't find a match, we'll either call the recipient and get the correct shipping address, or ask the client for an update. In any case, we work hard to make sure that we don't waste our client's money or reputation by shipping gifts to the wrong address.

- **Timing**. We bake our cookies in the morning and ship in the afternoon. Because we don't put any preservatives, corn syrup or shortening to extend their shelf life, they're best consumed in a week or less. We pay attention to shipping days and destinations to help deliver the freshest product possible. For example, we have a company that sends office gifts to dentists. Since most dental offices are closed on Friday – we don't ship gifts after Tuesday so they won't sit around over the weekend.

I read Keith Ferazzi's book, 'Whose got your back' a year ago, and it really resonated with me, personally and in our business. We've cultivated relationships over the years with suppliers who have our back. In turn, we treat all of our customers with the same philosophy. It's not something I do to get repeat business, but rather it is a way of life. I sleep a lot better at night knowing that when the oven gets turned off, I've finally answered the last email and setup everything for the next day, we've delivered exactly the kind of service we expect from others.

If this sounds like the type of service you'd like to get from a company that is sending personalized corporate gifts with your name on them, and you are not a customer of Anna's Gourmet Goodies, then maybe you should be. And if you are already sending gourmet cookie gifts from Anna's Gourmet Goodies, you can relax, we've got your back.

Life

"Your work is going to fill a large part of your life, and the only way to be truly satisfied is to do what you believe is great work. And the only way to do great work is to love what you do. If you haven't found it yet, keep looking. Don't settle. As with all matters of the heart, you'll know when you find it."

- Steve Jobs

Time is a valuable and important ingredient

Original Post Date: June 28, 2017

I believe it's true that as we get older, we think more about time. I can remember all the people who would tell me how 'time flies' when it comes to raising children. It was important enough for me to choose it as a word to focus on for the year - in life and in business. We can't change the quantity of time we have, but we can change the quality of how we spend it.

I started publishing OutsideTheOven.com almost nine years ago. One of my competitors back then (they've since closed down) started a blog that was titled something like 'as the cookie crumbles'. I liked the idea, but wanted to focus on something a bit different. My first post was about a river trip with Anna and a chance encounter with a snake.

I wanted to share something about myself, our company and what we do that doesn't involve flour, chocolate, butter, sugar and eggs – the ingredients we use to make cookies and brownies. I thought that if I shared more about who we are and what we've learned, it might help us make an emotional connection with customers and inspire our customers to do the same with their clients.

2008   2017

This Father's Day, I had the chance to once again spend the day on a river (thanks to the Haw River Canoe and Kayak Co. for a great experience) with Anna and it was the perfect way to spend an afternoon. No snakes this time, but I did spend some time in thought about the journey we've been on and why I started down this road in the first place. Stepping off the bus at SciQuest back in 2003 to venture down the road less traveled required a lot of thought and a major leap of faith.

My word for 2017 is 'time' – a culmination of lots of small moments. I've spent a fair amount of energy this first half of the year, thinking about how I spend my time both at home and with Anna's Gourmet Goodies. It is, after all, the only resource we can't acquire more of.

Running a business and raising a child have similarities in that they both require an extraordinary amount of time. Anna was off to college last year and while the quantity of day to day time requirements went down, it still requires thinking time and those moments when we did connect were all the more valuable.

At Anna's Gourmet Goodies, we spend our time (days and weeks and years) creating brief moments for our business clients and their customers. Our cookie gifts are impactful, connecting one person to another and creating a memorable moment when they open the package. We've developed some very efficient processes for managing orders, but we still spend a few moments thinking about each one and how it might impact our customer and the recipient. It's one ingredient that we think makes all the difference.

My Father's Day gift was time on the river with Anna and a delicious meal at the Saxapahaw General Store. The pizza with field grown tomatoes, fresh mozzarella and basil was simply outstanding, but the value of the time with Anna was priceless.

When we returned home, Anna presented me with a letter she wrote, thanking me and reminding me of some of the other times when we took small road trips. Little things that when stitched together add up to something greater than simply minutes on a clock.

Over the past few weeks I've spent time at Anna's Gourmet Goodies doing what we do throughout the year. Sending out birthday gifts for clients, a special batch of graduation party favors for a long time customer, thanking a business owner's clients for their recent purchase, and more. Little things that create moments to make someone's day a little brighter.

Outside the oven, I helped a friend repair his front porch so his wife could get into the house when she returned from the hospital, helped a college student service his car, and took this river trip with Anna.

As a husband, father and business owner, I'm always thinking about how I should be investing my time. It's a precious commodity that's made up of more than just minutes, hours and days. Focusing on that word this year has reminded me that it's helpful every now and then to step back, get outside the oven and look at the moments we're investing into relationships, a business, products or whatever.

Just like baking great cookies, you have to make sure you're adding the right ingredients in the right amount. Based on the last cookie I tasted and watching Anna grow and develop, I'm pretty happy with how things have turned out so far.

My visit to thank our first customer took me to a place I'd never been before

Original post date: May 17, 2016

I was inspired to share this story after thinking about it for more than a year. I strive to live, as much as possible, in a state of gratitude despite the daily barrage of circumstances that make up life. The fact that you are reading this book is the sum product of many people that have helped and encouraged me along my journey, and I suspect that if you sit and reflect, you'll have the same experience. For all of them, I am grateful. We live a richer life when we are grateful. Life and business for any of us can turn on a dime. While I can't really comprehend his circumstances, I felt compelled to make an extra effort to extend my gratitude to the person whose belief in me is a part of why you are reading this book right now.

Like most business owners, when someone asks the question, 'So, how did you start your business?' I love the opportunity to tell the story. For some people, starting a business is quick, like turning on a light switch. For some, it involves a story that starts long before the first customer appears. I had the chance to sit down with the first Anna's Gourmet Goodies customer recently, the one who helped launch our business, in an unusual setting. Our story starts with a cheesecake, not cookies, long before this first customer appeared.

I was working at SciQuest during the 'dotcom days' of the late 90's and early 2000's. Work was fast paced, constantly changing and investor money flowed like water from a garden hose. We worked hard, played hard, and had fun with some interesting events. One of those was the 'Cheesecake Bakeoff'.

I had baked a few cheesecakes over the years, all based on my Mom's recipe that I got from her over-stuffed box of food-stained index cards. It was made with eggs sugar and cream cheese, but included a sour cream topping, lightly baked, and adding a tang not found in traditional cheesecakes.

The night before the contest, I made a last minute decision to enter. While I knew the recipe was good, I wanted top prize and figured I needed to kick things up a notch. I made a crust with graham crackers and finely chopped dates. I diced up some apples, sautéed them lightly in Kentucky Bourbon, and layered that on top of the crust. I poured in the cheesecake mixture, baked it and added the sour cream topping. Finally, I whipped up a bourbon caramel sauce and drizzled it on top.

It looked great and I felt the addition of a little alcohol might give me an edge. As it turns out, I was right. My Apple Bourbon Cheesecake was crowned Grand Champion. I was awarded bragging rights and a baseball cap that I still have to this day. After winning, the recipe stayed dormant, for a while.

Months passed and after repeated encouragement to sell the cheesecake, I finally decided to see what it would take to bake and sell them. I contacted the NC Department of Agriculture and the Town of Wake Forest, secured permits and inspections, and we were set to start baking. But first, we needed the most important ingredient, a customer.

I had been eating lunch at a small café in Cary called Chef John's. As a somewhat regular patron, I got to know the owner, Chef John, and decided to ask him if he would give the cheesecake a try. He agreed.

I rounded up packaging from a local store, baked one cheesecake and dropped it by the restaurant. I checked back with Chef John after a few days and he said people 'Loved it!' So we made another. Then another. Then another.

From that one customer, we grew the business organically, adding new cheesecakes and eventually pies, finding customers who were willing to pay for our products to finance the growth. It grew until we decided in 2003 to take a leap of faith and build Anna's Gourmet Goodies full time.

We continued to grow our customer base and Chef John was a customer even after he closed the café and focused strictly on catering. But his business and his career, ended in January 2011 when he was arrested and charged with murder for the death of his wife.

Both Debbie and I made deliveries and got to know his wife Donna as well as Chef John. The news story was a shock to both of us. He was tried, convicted, and sentenced to life in prison.

It was the first time I was this close to someone convicted of this type of crime. It wasn't something I'd ever connect with Anna's Gourmet Goodies and our customers. I thought about him off and on over the years, but it wasn't until my neighbor interviewed me for his research project on hiring offenders that I began thinking of visiting Chef John.

Keith is a retired Federal prison warden and was completing his PhD. "It was never my job to judge whether or not anyone was right or wrong", he said. "I just did my job". It took a while, but at some point I felt compelled to track down Chef John, reach out, reconnect and thank him for what he did that was good, help me start Anna's Gourmet Goodies.

With Keith's help, I looked him up in the North Carolina prison directory and found he had been transferred to the Albemarle Correctional Institute. After calling, sending him a letter and completing the necessary forms to apply for a visit, I scheduled a trip to visit him on a Sunday afternoon.

It was my first visit inside a Federal Prison and not at all like what I've seen in the movies. The guards were firm, but friendly and the grounds were immaculate. After passing through security, I was sent to a large open room with tables and chairs to wait. A few minutes later, Chef John came out.

He had a big grin on his face, gave me a warm welcome and immediately asked about our cheesecakes and his favorite, our Key Lime Pie. We sat down and started catching up. If not for the surroundings, we might as well have been sitting back at the Café talking about old times.

I shared news about our business and how we had changed to only making cookies and brownies. I updated him on my family, as Anna was in a car seat when we first started deliveries to the Café. I asked about his life in prison and he filled me in on some of the details of his life behind bars.

We did not talk about the details of the event that led him there. That's not why I came. My visit was not about judgment, but gratitude and closure.

I try very hard to tie the threads of my stories back to Anna's Gourmet Goodies in a way that makes sense and provides you, the reader, with some measure of value. To give you food for thought that might inspire you to action in your life and/or business. And, to help our customers, both current and future, better understand the ingredients that make up our business beyond butter, flour, sugar and eggs. This one has been more than a little difficult, but no less important.

For me, it was a chance to say thank you to someone who, despite his current circumstance, helped me along my journey. In turn, I had the opportunity to help Chef John remember back to an earlier time and smile, if even for a brief moment. As I've written before, that's fundamentally what we do at Anna's Gourmet Goodies – create memories and hopefully generate a smile or two. Since the prison system would not allow me to do that with a cookie or a slice of pie, I used my words, a smile and a handshake. All of which make up a winning recipe for a brief moment of happiness, no matter how you slice it.

Thank you, Chef John.

This 'Foodie Connection' has been in the oven for awhile

Original post date: October 6, 2015

When I was at Duke's Fuqua School of Business I remember listening to remarks by J.B. Fuqua one day, and he said something that was not necessarily profound, but stuck with me all these years. He said that "If you are going to be successful in business, you've got to answer your phone". For me, I took that to mean that you never know how a connection to someone might turn out to be helpful in the future. Like all of us, I've made my share of connections along the way that turned out to be dead ends, but for the most part I am continually amazed at how often a chance encounter comes back to me later in life. Knowing what I know now, making and keeping quality connections is something that is increasingly more valuable.

If you spend any time at all around people in the food business, you'll understand they share two common traits; a passion for what they do and a love for connecting to others who share that passion. The road we've taken at Anna's Gourmet Goodies is full of people we've met along the way who've helped us, shared their knowledge and cheered us on. In turn, we've had the opportunity to do the same for others we've met. One of those opportunities to cheer someone on is my connection to Fanny Slater that began more than a dozen years ago when I first met her Dad, Jeff.

I was introduced to Jeff through a contact at my last employer who met him at his previous employer, GoodMark Foods. GoodMark purchased Jeff and his wife's company in 1989.

Ra El started Rachel's Brownies back in 1975. Jeff joined her in 1978 and together they grew the company to a nationally recognized brand. They appeared on TV shows such as The Phil Donahue Show and Charlie Rose, were featured in The New York Times and USA Today, and were even invited to the White House to have lunch with President Ronald Regan.

But the business wasn't born out of a desire to build a brownie empire. It was born out of a passion for chocolate and a desire to share that with the world. It just so happens that they made incredible brownies.

Jeff and I shared several conversations about what was then our wholesale dessert business. He was generous with his experience and we kicked around ideas for collaboration. At one point, he invited us down to Wilmington to have dinner with his family while they were vacationing. His daughters, Fanny and Sarah served as babysitters for the day, playing with Anna on the beach while the adults talked about life and business.

While we never launched a formal partnership, we've stayed in touch over the years. I recently reached out to get advice on a new idea I was working on and once again, Jeff was helpful in sharing his perspective and wisdom. I follow him on his blog, The Marketing Sage, and when I heard about Fanny and the Rachael Ray Cookbook Competition, I was excited to watch her pursing her passion for food and for the opportunity to cheer her on.

Encouraged by her Grandmother, and of course her parents, Fanny entered Rachael Ray's Great American Cookbook Competition along with nearly 1,000 other hopefuls. She made it from the top 20, to the top 10, to the top 5 which came with a phone call from Rachael herself and an invitation to compete for the grand prize of a cookbook contract on The Rachael Ray Show. Not only would the finalists cook in front of Rachael Ray, but some of the world's most renowned chefs including Jacque Pepin – a foodie's dream come true for sure.

I watched Fanny on several of the episodes and while I am a bit partial due to my connection, I can tell you that her authenticity and passion for food came through like a beacon.

It was not just about winning the contest, but about sharing her stories about food and family with the world. It was about pouring out her passion and making connections to others who share that same love of food and family. You can follow along and read more about her story on her blog at FannySlater.com Her cookbook Orange, Lavender & Figs is now available for pre-order on Amazon and due out on March 1st, 2016, so be sure and stay tuned.

Recently, Fanny agreed to sample some of our goodies and put together a video about her experience trying our products. I must admit that it was a little intimidating to send brownies to the daughter of the creator of a national brand. But I know that whether or not we come close to her Mom's recipe, I'm confident that we share some of the same measures of passion in our recipe.

Anna and I ventured down to Wilmington to share a meal with Fanny and re-connect after all these years. The last time they met, Fanny was about Anna's age and Anna was the girl in the sunglasses, running and playing in the sand. It is such a thrill to watch these two young women, one in the middle of living her dream and the other on the verge of venturing out to find her way in the world.

Fanny   Anna

Shady since 1985   Future's so bright...

There are a lot of reasons why we started Anna's Gourmet Goodies back in 2001. Of course we strive to be a profitable company and good stewards of what we've been given. But the real reason comes back to passion and time for family.

Our cookies and brownies are memorable gifts to anyone who has ever received a package from us, but the real gift for me has been the opportunity to build a business based on a passion to make others happy. Along with that, I've had the opportunity to spend time as a family and watch Anna on her journey, helping her find her passion, just as Fanny has done with hers.

We're on track to having our best year ever at Anna's Gourmet Goodies as connections to customers who believe what we believe has grown at a pace that continues to make us smile. Our passion for creating a memorable experience continues unabated. As we head into the busy season, we'll be busier than ever keeping up with orders, making sure that everything arrives just as expected, while welcoming new customers into the family.

We'll also keep our focus on nurturing those family and foodie connections, cheering on Fanny and Anna as they pursue their passions. It's what foodies do. After all, passion and connections are two of the most important ingredients in any recipe for a successful business and a wonderful life. Go Anna! Go Fanny!

I'm still using my word for the year

Original post date: October 6, 2015

I first learned about the concept of focusing on words from Chris Brogan. I've read books on focus, goal setting and time management. I've tried systems, checklists and applications. But I (and perhaps you) live in a world of relentless distraction. For me, choosing a single word serves as a lighthouse beacon, something that helps me get back to safety if I venture too far out, or avoid the rocks if I come too close to dangerous waters. If you've never tried it, I'd encourage you to give it a test drive. Don't wait until January, start today, right where you are.

If the Bradford pear trees in my neighborhood could speak and only say one word, it would be 'Spring!' Their white flowers are like trumpets, announcing the closing of the winter and the arrival of spring.

Those of us on Daylight Savings Time have moved our clocks forward and the turning of the calendar from 2014 to 2015 is in the distant past. Did you make any resolutions for the year? If you are like most people, they're long forgotten. I gave up on that practice a few years ago and adopted another method that is simple and actually sticks – a single word.

My friend Alan Hoffler of Millswyck Communications introduced me to the book, 'One Word Will Change your Life'. I used it last year and decided once again to pick a single word to focus on for the entire year in both my business and personal life. This year's word for me is 'Reach'.

It's both a noun and a verb. It's a word that propels me to take action. It might be as simple as extending a hand to say hello to a stranger. Helping a neighbor. Picking up a piece of litter. Or stretching myself to learn and master something new.

At Anna's Gourmet Goodies, it is at the core of what we do every day. We reach out to people on behalf of others. We send them a gift of our cookies and brownies, sharing different messages depending on what the sender has to say. Sometimes it is a thank you, sometimes to extend sympathy, and sometimes just to say hello.

I was delivering some cookies to Crossroads Infiniti, one of our local customers, several weeks back and had the opportunity to strike up a conversation with one of their customers in the waiting room. This Mom, with toddler in tow, was waiting for her car to be serviced.

She shared the story of her husband, a Marine, and his deployment on an aircraft carrier. She did not have or share a lot of detail, but enough to know that he was in harm's way in a part of the world more dangerous that I'll probably ever know. He loved our cookies and enjoyed getting them any time he visited the dealership's service department.

I immediately saw this as an opportunity to extend our reach. I asked for his address and shared my intent with Paul the General Manager. He agreed that sending this Marine cookies was the right thing to do. I wrote him a letter, describing my conversation with his wife, included it with a fresh batch of cookies, and packed everything up for shipping.

It just so happened this was the day of the biggest snowfall we had this winter. Nothing compared to what folks in the Northeast experienced, but enough to shut down our town for the day. But the cookies were made and we needed for them to reach their destination.

I piled the few orders we had on a sled and started the trek to the Post Office. It's only about a mile or so from the bakery. While I might have been able to drive, it felt like the right way to send off these orders. I stopped along the way to strike up a conversation with a veteran wearing his Vietnam War hat and shoveling snow. I listened to some of his stories. He immediately understood my mission, and I went on my way.

The Post Office gladly accepted our orders and sent them off to their respective destinations. About three weeks later, I received a wonderful email from the Marine, thanking me for the cookies. They had reached their destination, but more importantly, we were able to reach out and extend our thanks with a little taste of home to someone half way around the world serving our country.

In the past weeks, we've had the opportunity to reach out to employees of a security company and wish them a Happy Anniversary, to clients of a financial planner to say Happy Birthday, and to residents of apartment communities to thank them for calling their community 'Home'.

I keep a copy of my word posted above my desk as a reminder to look for opportunities to practice, every day. It's more than a 'To-Do' list or a long forgotten New Year's resolution – it's a reminder to reach out and focus on mental, physical, emotional and spiritual growth. If you've never picked a word and would like to give it a try, it's not too late.

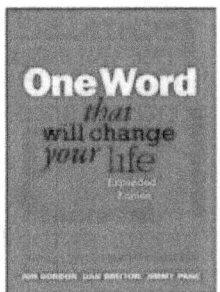

For Anna's Gourmet Goodies, it's about remembering that every single time we send something out the door, we are reaching out to someone, somewhere with a message and a gift that will hopefully bring them a brief moment of happiness. And that's a goal worthy of a little extra reach.

Why I'm really, really thankful this year

Original Post Date: November 24, 2013

Major life events have a way of sharpening our focus. The British writer Samuel Johnson was quoted as saying, "When a man knows he is to be hanged...it concentrates his mind wonderfully." Living in a state of gratitude can have a profoundly positive impact on our level of happiness and ultimately our own measure of success in life and business. I'd encourage you to think about sharpening your focus before having a life event.

It's official. The season of giving thanks and celebrating holiday traditions with friends and family officially begins this week. Yes, I know some retail stores put out Christmas decorations months ago – the real kick-off starts on Thursday.

At Anna's Gourmet Goodies we've been preparing for the 'holiday gift rush' over the past few months. We are grateful that many of our best and most loyal customers will be sending out our cookies again this year. We won't tally up numbers until the flour settles after we ring in 2014, but total sales are up nicely so far this year. We have you, our friends and customers to thank for that.

I believe that having an 'attitude of gratitude' is something that pays off in business and in your personal life. This past February I had the opportunity to get a clearer understanding of what that means on a personal level after taking a ride in the back of an ambulance to Rex Hospital.

I was finishing up my Valentine's Day grocery shopping after stopping by my doctor's office to make an appointment. I had not been feeling 100% and Debbie finally convinced me to go in for a visit. While at the store, a feeling came over me unlike anything I had ever experienced. I felt faint. My chest started to hurt. I knew things were not right. I dropped the basket, got in the car, and drove the 50 yards up the hill back to the doctor (I'm a practical guy – what can I say).

The urgent care office on the first floor took me in right away. When you say 'chest pain', you go to the front of the line. Within minutes, I was wired up, and people were rushing around. The doctor came in, took one look at the EKG and said, "Mr. Duke, you are going to the hospital right now. You are having a heart attack."

Within minutes, I was on a gurney, nitro under the tongue and on my way to the cardiac care unit in the ER. On a day filled with hearts, love and candy, I called Debbie from the back of the truck and said, 'Honey, meet me at the hospital. They tell me I'm having a heart attack. I'll be okay. I love you.'

To say that I received care that was over the top would be a gross understatement. From the EMTs who whisked me off to the hospital, to the staff ushering me into the ER, to the cardiologist who calmed me and diagnosed my issue with perfect precision, I was in the absolute best of hands.

Fortunately, it was not a heart attack or blockage. It did require minor heart surgery to remove fluid from around my heart. Once again, from the nursing team who cared for me, the prep-nurse, to the skilled surgeon and his team, I was cared for, prayed for and watched over with divine grace – no question about it.

The surgery was a complete success. After a few days in the hospital, I was given the all-clear to return home. Tests both in the hospital and afterwards revealed no problems. No treatments and no therapy. I recently completed a stress test and watched my heart pumping away on the 'heart TV' as I call it. Everything is functioning normally and according to my cardiologist, I have no more risk than the healthiest people on the planet.

Am I thankful this year? You bet I am. Not only is Anna's Gourmet Goodies having a good year, but I was given a rare gift – the chance to look at my life from a totally different perspective. To put my trust in the hands of an incredibly skilled and passionate group of people who were totally focused on giving me the chance to continue on my journey. To come out of the experience in near perfect health. The words 'thank you' really are not big enough.

I've said it before – we make cookies – but we are really in the business of making people happy. Of helping others say thank you to friends, family, clients, whomever. We've always been passionate about putting the same level of care in every order – whether it is one cookie or three thousand. However, this year I'll probably toss in an extra measure of thanks to share a little bit of the gift I was given this past February. You might not taste it in the cookies and brownies, but rest assured there's a little extra 'thank you' in every box.

What's in your 'mental' garden?

Original Post Date: April 20, 2012

Ideas are like plants - they must be cared for. And sometimes, they must be pruned. In life and in business, if we are cultivating our mind properly, we'll have some ideas that grow and flourish, and some we'll need to get rid of entirely. The most important thing to remember is that we must continue to cultivate the one organ in our body that makes us human - our mind.

Mary, Mary, quite contrary,
How does your garden grow?
With silver bells, and cockle shells,
And pretty maids all in a row.

It' springtime here in Carolina and my herb garden and surrounding plants are starting to strut their stuff. While I probably don't take as much time away from the oven or the keyboard as I should, I do enjoy looking at the plants up close as they begin to transform themselves without the least bit of help from me. Some things we've planted have died, while others keep coming back year after year.

We prune things back a bit, move some around from time to time, and sometimes we try new things, giving them room to grow. I'm thinking the same rules should apply to things called 'ideas' that we plant in the garden of our mind.

An idea, like a flower or an herb, is really an amazing thing. Some provide wonderful health benefits. Some are just pretty to watch. And some are harmful and should be avoided (i.e. I won't be growing any poison ivy in my garden). If we expect to have a bountiful garden, then we have to take the time to plant and nurture those ideas that are helpful, and give them room to grow. And when things don't work out, we have to set aside our fears, take out the pruning shears and get to work.

It is okay for different people to have different types of gardens. I watched an interview recently with Elizabeth Gilbert, the best-selling author of the book, 'Eat, Pray, Love'. She spoke of her mother and how she planted a 'Depression Era' garden where everything had a purpose and a place. Her garden on the other hand, was one she described as having 'indefensible beauty'.

Having a business like Anna's Gourmet Goodies has provided me the opportunity to cultivate my mental garden with all kinds of ideas. (Thankfully, Debbie has learned to tolerate my cultivation habits). Some have worked, while others have wilted, but I try to actively tend to the things I plant.

I was at a networking event the other night and someone asked me about our business, how we were doing in this economy, and what ideas I was working on. It made me think for a moment of Elizabeth's quote about indefensible beauty.

In our last newsletter, we included a note and a special offer to help us send cookies to raise money for Annalise Pelton as a part of a St. Baldrick's Event. Some of you responded, and we sent up a large bucket to be auctioned, along with some packages made special with her picture and logo. We posted a photo of her angelic smile on our Facebook page. Priceless.

About a week later, Annalise finally lost her battle with cancer.

The memory of that photo, the idea that maybe, for a brief moment, what we do at Anna's Gourmet Goodies made this little girl smile, is one that I'll be tending in my mental garden for the rest of my days. I may not always tell this story when someone asks about our business because it is sometimes difficult to share, but you can be sure that it is well rooted in my mental garden.

We've been working on some new ideas in the bakery for gluten free products. It's early in the process, but there is a possibility that we may have a product someday. When my neighbor, who suffers from a severe gluten allergy, tasted the cookie for the first time, it actually brought a tear to her eyes. "Do you know how long it's been since I've had something this good?"

The idea that our cookies make people happy is not some clever marketing idea, it is the foundation of what we do. And when I take time to cultivate new ideas in my mental garden, I'll do so with the idea of creating indefensible happiness among our customers. Now that's an idea worth nurturing.

How much does stress weigh?

Original Post Date: September 1, 2008

This is a short post, but is still as relevant today as ever. We all carry around more 'stuff' than ever, whether it is physical goods or thoughts. It's a good idea to stop every now and then and spend some time thinking about how much the load we are carrying really weighs and whether or not it is worth it.

The true weight of stress depends on how long you hold it

The day that we set aside to honor our American workers whose labor has contributed to the strength, prosperity and well-being of our economy has come and gone. Labor Day marks the unofficial end of summer vacation and is often the last big weekend for getting the family outdoors. We spent the afternoon at the pool, enjoying some warm sun and a chance to finish a little reading while the kids splashed and played in the water.

Unless you have been living in a cave for the past 6-9 months, you probably agree that we are going through a rough patch in our economy right now. Whatever part of the labor force you participate in, you may have experienced or noticed an increase in stress among your peers. I hear a lot of people talking about stress at work and how tough business is for them right now. And although Anna's Gourmet Goodies has enjoyed brisk growth during this time, we still face some of the same challenges other businesses face, most notably the rapid increase in material costs.

I was thinking of stress and water, because my wife handed me a copy of a story she had tucked away in a book titled,

"Put the glass down". It seems that a professor held up a glass of water and asked his class how much it weighed. Answers ranged from an ounce to a pound. He explained that it was not that absolute weight that he was interested in, "It depends on how long you hold it". You see, if you hold up a glass of water for a minute, the weight does not matter. If you hold it up for an hour, it gets a little heavier and your arm will hurt. If you hold it up for a day, you'll probably need an ambulance to take you to the hospital. The weight of the glass did not change, but it became heavier the longer you hold it.

It seems that burdens and the stress associated with them have the same properties. If we carry them around all the time, they eventually get too heavy to bear. It's vital to put them down and get some rest, so that we can carry on.

On this long weekend, I hope that you had the opportunity to lay your burdens and stress down for at least a little while. This story was a reminder that I need to give myself permission to put things down from time to time. They'll either be there waiting for me when I'm ready to pick them up again, or I might just realize that they really were not worth carrying around anyway.

A look back in time

Original Post Date: April 17, 2009

I have many memories of growing up and hearing stories from my parents and relatives about what life was like during the time when they grew up. While I'm sure I 'rolled my eyes' occasionally as a teenager, I realize now just how important it is to share lessons with young people about how things were done in the past. There was a time before the Internet and Smartphones. Understanding where we came from is important in preparing us for the journey ahead.

I don't drive a DeLorean, but we did manage to take a short trip back in time last weekend. The North Carolina Work Horse and Mule Association hosted their Annual Corn Planting Day at Indian Ridge Farm in Linden, NC and we headed out for an afternoon of family fun. It was a short drive from Wake Forest, but it felt as though we had traveled years back in time.

The association is made up of a group of folks that are interested in preserving our farming heritage by educating people about the use of animals to plow the fields and plant the crops as it was done in the early 1900's. There was a display of antique tractors, but they sat silently beside the split rail fence. They took a back seat to the sounds of mules braying, farmers calling out commands to the teams, and the sound of metal slowly turning the earth over, preparing for the fertilizer and then the seed.

Like any proper gathering on a farm, there was a lunch line with homemade cakes, cookies, hot dogs, chili and other edibles. Old time music floated gently through the air on a sunny afternoon. One group, Washboard Ray and Little

Sidney presented their version of the variety show, complete with a washtub bass, good humor and family style stories. At nine years old, Sidney looks to have a promising career in the entertainment field and Ray was a treat as he narrated the show.

Anna tried her hand at helping distribute the fertilizer in the field. She guided the plow while the team of horses trod slowly back and forth across the field. Several other kids and adults got their turn at walking behind the team. It was entertainment for today, but a way of life that has mostly disappeared from our landscape.

While they were planting corn, it did give me pause to think about Anna's Gourmet Goodies and how we rely on a farmer, somewhere, to care for the earth, till the soil, plant the wheat, and hope that nature responds with bounty. As I watched those men and women skillfully maneuvering their teams around the field, it reminded me just how our farmers put their livelihood at risk, to produce the food we so easily acquire every day at the local grocery.

With all the greed, gluttony, fraud and abuse that dominate the news these days, it was refreshing to step back and mingle with those men and women who till the dirt and plant their hopes and dreams several times a year. They are careful stewards of the land that provides them a life and feeds at least a part of the world. I did not hear a single word about bad mortgages, foreclosures, bankruptcy, bailouts, mergers, or layoffs all day. It was indeed a breath of fresh air.

I hope that Anna came away with a little more appreciation of just how the materials we buy for our business and the food for our table, gets started in the first place. Somebody has to till the dirt and plant the seeds to produce the crop that eventually, becomes one of our cookies or brownies. I'm just grateful that I had the opportunity to spend an afternoon with some of these folks and learn a little bit about our farming heritage in the Sandhills of North Carolina.

I am reminded of this version of an ancient Chinese proverb I heard on public radio about 25 years ago:

When the sun comes up, I go to work.
When the sun goes down, I take my rest.
I dig the well from which I drink,
I till the soil from which I eat.
Kings can do no more.

Business

"Running a business is like white water rafting. You're in a raft with other people you need to depend on. Sometimes you drift in calm waters. Sometimes you find yourself in a raging current. Someone has to steer, and the others have to paddle. You pick a path and work towards the goal of having fun and everyone making it to the end. But someone will probably fall into the water and occasionally, you get stuck on a rock."

- Chris Duke

Business lessons from a Burgermaster

Original Post Date: April 12, 2017

One of my favorite quotes is from Bill Nye, The Science Guy. "Everyone knows something you don't". When it comes to business, it is a universal certainty. It's one of the reasons I'm constantly looking to learn from others, whether or not I'm in the same business. Some principles and truths are universal, and in this case, knowing who you are and what you are really good at are clear reminders of what makes businesses successful over the long term.

Being in the specialty foods industry for nearly 16 years has given me a different perspective on food and the people who help make it. I have admiration for the large companies, like Chobani, who churn out millions of units of their products every day as well as chefs like David Mao at David's Noodle Bar, who lovingly hand rolls his famous pork dumplings, one at a time.

Anna was home for spring break and we decided to take a road trip to visit a small lunch spot in Siler City, named by OnlyInYourState.com as 'The Best Burger Joint' in the state. It was about a 90 minute ride, but spending the afternoon with my daughter while searching for burger nirvana ranks up there as the perfect way to spend an afternoon for me.

We arrived at Johnson's Drive In just before the lunch rush and a line had already formed. One line for take-out and one for dine in. It's a small place by today's standards. A dozen stools at the counter and about six booths all covered in green leatherette – it feels like stepping back in time, in a good way.

The place was busy for sure, but there was no feeling of anyone being rushed. Johnson works the grill like a master conductor with skills only time and experience can produce. The waitress attends to each of the diners, welcoming 'outsiders' like us, as well as regulars who don't even need to order – she knows.

The menu is on the wall above the grill, no need for printed paper in this place. I think I remember seeing an option for hot dogs, but I'd be surprised if Johnson sells more than a few every now and then. People come here mostly for one thing – cheeseburgers. I struck up a conversation with another traveler who made a detour to stop in that day. He recommended the cheeseburger all the way with homemade chili, slaw, onions and mustard.

We were seated at a booth and the waitress came by to take our order – cheeseburger all the way, fries and a sweet tea. If you are going to sample the best of Southern cuisine, this is a must.

Burgers are cooked to order, so it takes a few minutes longer than your typical fast food variety. But when she delivered them in a sheet of waxed paper, they were piping hot. I mustered up the self-restraint to stop for a couple of quick photos, then carefully bit into Johnson's hand crafted masterpiece. It was so good, I actually got goose bumps.

Wanting to take in the full experience, we decided to try a slice of Chocolate Pie from the menu. The waitress apologized, but they were all out. "I could bring you another burger" Sold.

We savored every bite, taking in not only the food but the atmosphere. The burgers were good to be sure, but Johnson's was more than that for me, it was an experience, something we focus on every day at Anna's Gourmet Goodies. Watching the customers, the staff and the Burgermaster himself gave me pause to think about our cookie business and what I might learn from someone who has been doing basically the same thing for nearly 71 years.

Here are a few of my observations:

Made from scratch

Claxton Johnson starts his day early in the morning when a delivery truck comes by with full sides of Western grain-fed

USDA Choice beef. He picks out only the best beef, and then grinds it fresh into portions for the day's burgers. No frozen, pre-made patties here.

We pick up our flour from Lindley Mills, crack fresh eggs, and mix each batch of cookies adding one ingredient at a time. No pre-mix in our bakery.

A well-defined business

Johnson's Drive In is open Tuesday thru Saturday from 10 a.m. until 2 p.m. No nights, no mornings. No telephone to call in orders. No credit cards. No expanded seating or second location. When the day's meat is all cooked, he shuts down the grill.

We operate our business via AnnasGourmetGoodies.com. We bake and ship cookies Monday thru Friday throughout the year, with some exception made during the Holiday Season. We have no plans to open a store or distribute cookies via retailers.

Do one thing really well

Claxton Johnson makes great cheeseburgers. His hamburgers are good and I'm sure the hot dogs are as well. But cheeseburgers are his masterpiece.

We make chocolate chip cookies. Our oatmeal raisin cookies, brownies and shortbread are all very good, but our chocolate chip cookies are outstanding.

As we stood up to leave, I took in one last look around, watching the master at work on the grill and at the lunch counter. I started to edge over and tell him about our experience, but I decided not to break his stride. He knows.

In his book The Outliers, Malcolm Gladwell talks about the 10,000 hours required to master a skill. Claxton Johnson passed that mark long before I was born. And I like to think we've passed that mark making our gourmet cookie and brownie gifts a while back as well.

I love to seek out other artisans and masters in the food world to see what I can learn from them. While I don't expect to ever be in the cheeseburger business, I walked away with more than a full stomach and a smile, feeling as though I spent a little time in the presence of a master of his craft. That's the feeling we strive to create every time someone bites into our chocolate chip cookies. Goosebumps would also be nice.

We're in the H2H business

Original Post Date: November 21, 2016

Of all the presentations I've been to at conferences, this was one of my favorites. It struck a chord with me because it was a simple concept that any business can use to change the focus for the better. Stop thinking about B2B or B2C. If your business relies on human beings as customers, then you are in the Human to Human business.

I've been going to the Internet Summit in Raleigh every year since it began. It's a chance to not only hear from thought leaders and rock stars in the digital world, but to network with peers who are interested in learning more about the technologies that have infiltrated and changed our lives forever.

Anna's Gourmet Goodies has been on the web since 2002. We've evolved over the years, allowing me to combine my technology skills and background with a passion for creating products that feed people's soul. I love meeting people who know something I don't and are willing to share that knowledge. One of the people I met this year is Melanie from Sisarina.

Melanie has a gift for engaging the audience with her authenticity and passion. Her company, Sisarina, is named after her imaginary childhood friend. I was drawn to her topic, which was different than some of the heavy technology being shared that day, "Rock Your Business – Stop Selling. Build a Club."

She used the example of Mini Cooper cars and how their marketing is focused not so much on the cars themselves, but the people who drive them. Apparently driving a Mini means you're in the club. You wave at other drivers. You go on adventures instead of drives. It's not about steel, rubber and petroleum products, it's about the soul of the people behind the wheel.

Technology folks are famous for acronyms. I can't tell you how many surveys I've taken where they ask what kind of business we are at Anna's Gourmet Goodies. Are we a B2C (business to consumer) or B2B (business to business) Melanie challenged all of us that we are neither. "You see", she said, "We are all in the H2H business. Human to Human".

What a simple and profound concept. I immediately thought about a recent experience I had meeting a new friend from the Ukraine. I was at Crossroads Infiniti and Yuri (the sales manager) was speaking with a client in Russian. My Russian has faded to a few words, but Yuri introduced me to the customer, whose name was Yuriy. He had recently moved to the United States and was there with his wife and his infant son, also named Yuriy.

I was in no position to try and speak Russian, but Yuriy was kind enough to practice his English. We talked about his coming to the US and their experience starting a new life here. The conversation moved to Anna's Gourmet Goodies and our chocolate chip cookies. As an Infiniti customer, he absolutely loved them.

He described some of the cookies from the Ukraine and said that oatmeal raisin was very popular there and one of his favorites. He shared other treats and things about his culture.

He was incredibly kind, respectful and I thoroughly enjoyed meeting him and his family.

Afterwards, I asked Yuri (the sales manager) to send me his address. I baked up a couple of packages of our oatmeal raisin cookies and sent them to Yuriy and his wife along with a brief note. I welcomed him to the US and confirmed what he already knew, that Yuri and the other people at Crossroads Infiniti were not just professionals, but really good human beings.

About a week later, I was in the dealership and Yuriy (from the Ukraine) was there with his wife and infant. He had brought in a bag of candies from Russia for me. He walked up and with a huge grin on his face, hugged me and thanked me profusely for my kindness. All I did was send him a few cookies, but it was clear that the impact and connection went way beyond that. I was overwhelmed and even got a little misty.

We send out cookie and brownie gifts to people every day. We hope the connections we make generate this type of reaction from the people who receive them. But we rarely get a chance to experience this side of the human connection. It had an impact on how I view our business.

Sadly, not everyone has heard Melanie's message and understands they are in the H2H business. We lost an order this week to a technology company who is stuck in the B2B business. The admin, who prepared the gift list, sent us the order without a person's name for the packages, only a company. These were going to large companies and I asked if they were sure they wanted to do this. She said yes.

From our experience, we knew the packages would be delivered, but we would likely get a phone call from the recipients asking who the packages were for. The opportunity for the technology company sending the gifts, to make a human connection to their customer, would be lost. When I asked a second time, just to be sure, they went with another large cookie company who will simply take their money and ship the order.

I can't think of a time when it is more important to be reminded that we are in the human to human business. Things get busy this time of year. We'll be working hard to hand craft our cookie and brownie gifts, and make sure they get to the right destination.

But thanks to Melanie and Yuriy, no matter how busy we get, we'll remember that we are not sending cookie and brownie gifts to an address or a business. We're sending them to a human being. And if we create even a small measure of happiness and gratitude that I saw in Yuriy's face and felt in his hug, then I'll sleep well knowing we've hit our goal by creating something that lasts long after the package is empty – a human connection.

Traditions are part of our family and our business

Original Post Date: November 2, 2016

The word 'tradition' is often associated with family, however, it has equal importance in business as well. Traditions create memories and that can be a good thing in any business. It might be traditions that are focused on employees or customers. In either case, spending time focusing on creating opportunities to develop traditions is worth the investment.

We're entering the season of traditions. In a few weeks, people across America will gather with friends and family to give thanks and share a meal centered around turkey, dressing, cranberries, pumpkin pie and a host of other comfort foods that are part of their Thanksgiving tradition.

Following that, we'll celebrate traditions again in December. In my house it's Christmas, maybe it's Hanukkah in yours, or another tradition. These are big traditions, but sometimes the smaller ones in our families are just as important. We recently went to the NC State Fair as part of a tradition in our family that includes roots to the beginning of our business.

Growing up, my parents took me to the Kentucky State Fair. We didn't have phones with cameras to capture the images, but I have vivid memories of talking to Freddy Farm Bureau and the time I ate a corn dog and lost a tooth (no, we did not go on a mission to find it later). Memories from traditions are more permanent than anything digital.

Debbie and I started taking Anna to the NC State Fair from the time she was an infant. I'd take off an afternoon and we'd wander around the grounds looking at the booths, the animals, the vegetables and all the other stuff that comes with the State Fair. We'd park the stroller on a grassy hill (yes – it is still there) spread out a blanket and have a picnic with Anna.

When Anna was three, we stopped by the Village of Yesteryear where artisans and crafts people demonstrate skills from days gone by. We met Karl Johnson a scissor artist and decided to have him create a silhouette of Anna. Watching a skilled scissor artist work is truly an experience. His brother Erik now carries on the tradition of scissor art at the State Fair.

We framed the image and hung it on the wall in our office. When we started our company and named it Anna's Gourmet Goodies, I scanned the image and 15 years later we're still reminded that our brand was born out of a tradition.

This year, Anna found time to get away from college and come back home to go to the fair as a family. And, just as we have in years past, we followed our NC State Fair tradition. We stroll through the buildings, looking at the exhibits, stopping at least once at the House Autry booth for a fresh hushpuppy. We stopped for a quick photo in front of The Big Cart, a V8 powered shopping cart from the NC Department of Agriculture (I'm still negotiating for a chance to take it for a spin around the parking lot).

2007   2016

Then, we're off to my favorite corn dog vendor where they're hand-dipped and fried up fresh and hot. We explore the flower gardens, stop at the Village of Yesteryear and say hello to Erik and Dan Dye (a silversmith). We take a ride on the Ferris wheel, and finish off the night with some fresh made ice cream churned by John Deer tractor engines, while watching the fireworks. We've followed pretty much the same ritual every year.

Not everyone connects with a State Fair as an annual tradition. But for me, it is an experience that, despite whatever noise might be going on in the world at the time, reminds me that we live in a great country.

Do you have traditions in your family and/or your business? Looking back, it's clear to me that traditions are threads that bind us together. The cord we hang on to that gets us thru the ups and downs, the ebbs and flows of the year. A reminder that it is okay to pause, to celebrate and to remember.

At Anna's Gourmet Goodies, we have customers who order gifts from us once or twice, and we love that. We also have customers who've made sending our gifts a tradition. We're grateful to have the opportunity to provide not only our cookies and brownies, but in some small way, be part of a tradition that binds together our customers with the people they choose to share our gifts.

I hope you'll make some time to reflect on traditions, even small ones, in your family and your business. And if Anna's Gourmet Goodies happens to be a part of that tradition, know that we take that responsibility seriously and always strive to deliver more than simply great cookies and brownies, but an experience that has a lasting impact on every person who opens one of our packages. That's a tradition we're proud to be a part of.

This gift won't have our cookies - but it will be an experience

Original Post Date: September 22, 2016

The concept of focusing on creating an experience applies to many businesses. There are lots of bakeries, coffee shops, hotels, restaurants, etc. - but think for a moment about the ones you've visited or done business with that focused not just on the end product or service, but the entire experience. They are the businesses that leave lasting impressions and inspire people to share their story.

One of the best compliments you can receive from a customer is when they ask you for a referral. It is a signal that you have become, as my friend Chris Brogan calls it, an ally as opposed to simply a vendor looking to sell something. We had an opportunity to create something special for a customer recently and it was a true gift for us to be able to design an experience for their clients.

Our customer contacted us to provide a referral to another company for client gifts this holiday season. Not that they were unhappy with our products – it was just that they wanted something a little different. I took it as a supreme compliment they would ask my opinion on alternatives.

I looked around at some companies and sites to see what might fit. We know a few others out there who do some great work (like Berta Scott down at Southern Supreme in Bear Creek). After giving it some thought, knowing what we've learned about their company and how they treat their clients, we thought it might be interesting to see if we could create something beyond a gift and deliver an experience their clients would always remember.

We are fortunate to have some very talented food professionals in our area. Years ago I connected with Missy at LaFarm bakery in Cary. Her husband Lionel is a true rock star in the world of baking. In addition to running a thriving bakery, he lectures at conferences and his book, A Passion for Bread: Lessons from a Master Baker, says it all. His work flows from his passion.

I stopped in one day to discuss my idea of including some of his sweet breads in our gift and it was done. We'll be adding Lionel's coffee breads to our 'gift experience'.

Next, I wanted something to go with that and naturally, I looked for coffee. Coffee roasting has exploded right up there with craft beer and once again, I found a shop, Back Alley Coffee Roasters.

Beth and her husband Tracy started this business after an experience learning to roast coffee 'in a back alley' of sorts at the college where Tracy was a professor. They started, much in the same way as Lionel, out of a passion to create something wonderful. When you stand in their shop and watch the baristas create a custom pour over for customers, it's clear they understand the difference between producing a product and crafting an experience. We checked off another item with coffee from Back Alley.

Finally, we needed something to put the bread and the coffee in. A box or a tin just did not seem right. A wood crate would be a nice touch. I started looking for solutions out there, but couldn't find anything to fit our size and budget requirements. I did find one company that could have made the product, but after some thought, I decided to reach out to Richard.

Richard is retired and lives in Louisville. He began his career serving in the military and later went on to work at Fall City Brewery where he did a variety of jobs, including a tour guide. Richard loved to help people by building things and eventually ventured out on his own providing building and repair services.

Working on your own is never easy, especially when you have (5) children and a wife at home. But they worked together as a team, always doing the right thing for his customers, providing for the needs of his family, living responsibly and being faithful in charity to his church and community. His passion shows in his integrity and always wanting to do things right. He seemed like the perfect fit to craft the wooden crate to finish off our gift experience.

He agreed to let us use his workshop, so Debbie and I traveled to Kentucky to make some sawdust and craft some crates. The size of the order came in nearly triple what we initially expected, so we had a bit of work to do.

One of my favorite quotes is from Science Guy Bill Nye – "Everyone knows something you don't". It drives one of my passions, learning. Spending a weekend in the woodshop with a master craftsman like Richard was certainly an experience for me. We crafted the parts that would bring this project together.

The coffee breads, freshly roasted coffee and hand crafted crate came together nicely. To top it off and create the final piece of the experience, I put together cards with pictures of the craftspeople and their stories. In the end, we believe that creating an experience is more than just the taste of a product or the colors in the packaging, it is the story behind it and the feeling it evokes that make the difference. The recipients who get this package are in for an experience they'll not soon forget.

This project was a chance for us to learn things that we'll apply to gifts from Anna's Gourmet Goodies. While it is dangerous for a business to stray too far from their core mission, we felt this project fit nicely with our core mission I discussed some time ago in this post titled 'Real magic happens when you understand the why'.

We won't be shipping these out until the first of December as a part of our Holiday gift rush, but having the opportunity to work on a project like this has been like an early gift for us. Telling someone else's story is extremely gratifying.

By the way, in addition to being a generous craftsman, Richard is also my father in law. Not only did I get to spend time in the workshop and learn from a master, we were there to help him celebrate his 85th birthday. For me, that is a sweeter gift than anything coming out of our oven.

Our gourmet cookie gifts are 'sticky'

Original Post Date: April 11, 2016

One of the most read business books of all time is 'Made to Stick' by Chip and Dan Heath. It is the one thing that businesses universally seek to accomplish - to make products and create services that stick in the mind of their customers. While there is no magic formula to fit every circumstance, there are basics you can do to increase the chances of making your brand stick with customers.

No, I'm not referring to the kind of sticky that comes from putting your hand in the honey jar. I'm thinking about sticky as it relates to memory, something that stays there for a long time.

Anna and I watched the Disney movie 'Inside Out' (worth seeing if you have not) and it was an interesting take on what happens to our thoughts and memories. It was funny, well done as most Pixar movies are and got me thinking about what we do at Anna's Gourmet Goodies. We often describe our gifts as 'leaving a lasting impression long after the last crumb is gone'.

I also received a phone call recently from a former customer because we created a memory for her. One of her employers used to send our cookies as gifts to their employees. She decided to start sending gifts to her clients and called us because of that memory.

One of the first things she said was how she remembered getting our cookies on her birthday and work anniversary, a simple 'thank you' gift from her company letting her know she was valued and appreciated. This was years ago and I'm wondering, of all the things the HR department did, how many of them stood out like the simple gesture of remembering employees with a box of cookies on their birthday and work anniversary?

Jim Karrh, a friend and former classmate at Duke's Fuqua School of Business, is a consultant helping companies focus on managing the message they send to customers and employees. I subscribe to his email newsletter and he shared this story in a recent post:

> *"I see a widespread assumption among managers that the main way to improve productivity is to set tough goals and push people. Yet we're learning that employees who feel appreciated are more productive and loyal. An on-the-job study of 41 university fundraisers, all of whom were working on fixed salaries, confirmed this. For half of the group, the development director visited them in person to say, "I am very grateful for your hard work. We sincerely appreciate your contributions to the university." The other half of the group received no extra expression of thanks.*
>
> *What do you think happened? During the next week, the group who received direct thanks increased the number of calls*

they made by 50 percent, while the control group made the same
number of calls as they had the previous week."

— *Jim Karrh, Managing the Message*

Thinking about the movie, Jim's quote, our business, and my
own life, I believe two factors make a particular event or
experience memorable: the unexpected and emotional
connections.

It happens to all of us. We get caught up in the routine of life
and business. But then, when something unexpected
happens, either good or bad, we stop for a minute and that's
when the memory kicks in – like when someone gives us a
real, sincere, 'thank you', that is totally unexpected.

Another powerful memory generator happens when we make
an emotional connection. When I smell strawberries, I think
of Mom's strawberry cake she always made on my birthday.
When I say the words 'my daughter' I am transported back to
that dimly lit room where she came into the world and I saw
her for the first time. Both evoke emotions tied to permanent
memories. Do you have memories from emotional triggers? I
bet you do.

While I'm flattered when people refer to me as 'the cookie
man', (this happened just the other day at a Raleigh Chamber
luncheon), I smile knowing that we are really in the business
of creating 'sticky memories'. When someone opens the
package and bites into a cookie or brownie, I'd like to think
two things happen. First, they are pleasantly surprised. And
second, they are transported back to a time in their youth
when they sat around a plate of cookies their Mom or
someone special just made.

I have no way of confirming exactly how many of the tens of
thousands of packages we've sent out over the years created

an experience that ended up tucked away somewhere in the memory banks of the person who opened the box and tasted our cookies and brownies. But I can say with certainty that it did for the customer who called us recently, and probably a few more.

Sticky memories. For a company in the business of creating memorable experiences, that's a pretty sweet reward.

Why I stopped sending newsletters nearly two years ago

Original Post Date: August 30, 2015

Despite what you might read from some experts, email marketing is by no means dead. However, marketing in general has changed. While there are still plenty of 'in your face', 'buy-buy-buy' campaigns out there, consumers are more educated than ever before. Anything you want to know about a company can be found with a few clicks. People, especially millennials, are equally interested in knowing about the company vying for their business, in addition to the product or service. Sharing stories is one way to educate your customers.

August marks fourteen years since Debbie and I first incorporated the company that is now Anna's Gourmet Goodies. Like all businesses, we've had ups and downs, victories and defeat. Along the way, we've collected stories, relationships and experiences that will, hopefully, make it into the book someday. In the meantime, we strive to inspire you in some way, make you smile, or maybe even shed a tear. Whether you're a customer or someone who takes time to read this post, thank you.

It's been over two years since I stopped sending out a 'newsletter', opting instead to share brief stories about experiences that are relevant (sometimes loosely) to Anna's Gourmet Goodies. I've received more than a handful of comments and smiles from people who read the email, many of whom I had no idea were on the list. Our business has grown nicely these past two years, so I'll continue for now.

This month, I have two stories – one recent and one that while, not so recent, is an important part of understanding more about Anna's Gourmet Goodies and what drives our business.

I met Michael Davis, a customer at Crossroads Infiniti (one of our customers) during a routine visit to drop off some cookies. After noticing his Army cap (retired), I shook his hand and thanked him for his service. We struck up a conversation and he shared a part of his story.

He was in the Army Signal Corp. During one of his final deployments to Iraq, he had the opportunity to visit the hole where Saddam Hussein was captured and actually sat down with his feet dangling inside. As you might expect from his towering size, he did not go down inside. He was struck by the fact that someone who was at once so powerful, ended up tucked away in this tiny hole in the ground.

I have no idea how many people in the world have done this, but meeting Michael and hearing about his experience made my day and gave me something to think about. A reminder that everyone has a story, and unless you take time to ask, you might miss out on a good one.

When he left, I'm certain the service representative gave him a package of our cookies. A small gesture, but I hope that the cookies made by our hands served as another 'thank-you and left him with a brief moment of happiness.

One of my favorite stories is one that is difficult for me to tell without my voice cracking and my eyes starting to water. I've spoken about it many times to various groups, but it far easier to write.

We sent Annalise gifts on a few occasions when her Aunt Tracey ordered cookies from us to send to her. She told us Annalise's story, being diagnosed with Neuroblastoma while barely two years old. We sent her cookies once for her birthday, and included a mylar balloon and a stuffed animal (no, you won't find this on our website).

In 2012, Tracey sent us a note telling us that Annalise was going to be the featured child in a St. Baldrick's event in her hometown and wondered if we might send some cookies. Having fought the cancer bravely for 5 of her brief 7 years, we eagerly agreed, put together a label with her name and picture and sent out a large tin bucket of cookies to help raise money, along with a special package for Annalise. The only thing I asked for in return, was a picture.

I included a letter to Annalise, telling her how special we thought she was and how we would pray for her and ask God to give her time to do her work here on Earth. We never met, but I wanted her to know how special she was and that she inspired us with her spirit.

We made sure the cookies arrived shortly before the event. While we were not there, we understand it was a big success. The picture we received was more than enough reward for us.

On Sunday, March 18, the day after St. Patrick's Day and a few days after receiving our cookies, Annalise lost her battle with cancer. I wanted so much to put some magic ingredient in those cookies to cure her disease, but alas I could not. What I can do, is to keep her memory alive by telling her story, just as I am doing right now. Read more about her on this website, AnnalisesFriends.org.

It would be nice to think that of the hundreds of thousands of cookies and brownies we've sent out over the years have touched lives in a special way or inspired similar stories. Maybe. Maybe not. That's okay.

It's like the story of the small boy walking down a beach littered with starfish who tossed them one by one back into the ocean so they would not die. When asked why he did this, and told that he could not possibly make a difference, he picked up another starfish, tossed it back and replied, "It made a difference to that one!"

I share stories like these because I believe that in the case of people like Michael and Annalise, we all have the opportunity to make some small impact on the lives of customers, friends, family and strangers, even if for a brief moment.

Share a story. Listen to a story. Pass on a story. It matters. It's part of being human.

Sharing stories is important to us because it helps our customers (and perhaps future ones) understand who we are and why we do what we do. We can't say for sure, but with every package that leaves the bakery, it is our hope that the person who receives it will enjoy the work of our hands and at least for a brief moment, experience a memory that will become part of their life's story, whatever that may be.

A lofty goal, but it makes for a good ending to the story.

Bob Ross would have called this a 'happy accident'

Original Post Date: June 29, 2015

Some of the most well-known products in history were the result of accidents or discoveries that at first look, were not fit for one thing but turned out to be revolutionary. Ever used a 'sticky note'? No business on the planet will ever get it right all the time, but there are cases where it is possible to turn what might first appear to be a mistake, into something of value.

If you've spent any time watching PBS, you probably remember Bob Ross. Bob was a soft spoken, gentle soul who, in the span of 30 minutes, created landscape paintings with a blank canvas using brushes, a painting knife and his imagination. Nothing was every wrong in his world. If something didn't go just right, it was not a mistake but rather he referred to it as a 'happy accident'.

Despite our best efforts, not everything goes right in our bakery either. While we refuse to ship orders that are not as close to perfection as we can get, when things don't turn out quite right we try very hard not to waste anything. If a batch is not up to spec, or we are experimenting with a new recipe, we do our best to salvage the product and create our own version of a 'happy accident'. This is how we created Shepard's Shortbread.

A few years ago, we were making several batches of our Artisan Cookies. The bakery was humming, mixer going, cookie helpers forming the dough and sheets going into the cooler. In an attempt to keep the hopper full, I inadvertently added the flour to the butter and sugar mixture before adding the eggs. No way to reverse this.

Eggs not only provide moisture, but leavening as well. Without it, you have a basic shortbread recipe. I sat the dough aside and later rolled it out, cut it into squares and baked up some shortbread. It was really, really good.

Whenever we have extra cookies or are experimenting with a new recipe, we never like to see good product go to waste. One of our favorite places to visit and donate extra product, is The Shepherd's Table Soup Kitchen in Raleigh. They 'Serve the Hungry and Feed the Soul'. Right up our alley.

I carried the short bread down there and offered it up for their lunch. It was a hit and over the next few weeks we had a few more 'happy accidents' as we worked on getting the recipe and process just right.

After a few rounds of testing, we decided to add it to our Artisan Cookie Tower. We named it Shepherd's Shortbread in honor of our friends who serve those in our community in need of physical and spiritual nourishment.

A few weeks ago during one of our cookie making sessions, I inadvertently forgot to add the eggs again. This time, to our traditional cookie recipe. No problem – I set the dough aside knowing that this was just another 'happy accident'.

I baked up some shortbread and dropped it off at the Shepard's Table. Raven and Michael were more than happy to add it to the lunch menu. While I did not stick around for the lunch rush, I'm hoping that combined with the other food served up that day, the 'happy accident' from Anna's Gourmet Goodies helped feed the soul of the guests who dined with them that day. That's right in line with our mission.

Bob passed away on July 4th nearly 20 years ago. We never met, but something tells me that our version of a 'happy accident' would meet with his approval. And while everything we do might not turn out perfect, being of service and making people happy is always a key ingredient in our recipes.

Corbin, The Colonel, Our Cookies and his Creed

Original Post Date: January 29, 2015

Kentucky Fried Chicken consistently ranks in the top 100 globally recognized brands across a variety of indexes. And the story behind how that happened had a profound and lasting impact on my view of business and what it takes to succeed over the long term. There is a lesson in this brand for all types of businesses.

Any chef will tell you, it takes more than a list of ingredients to make something great. If you have ever had a pack of our cookies, you have a complete list of everything in them. But I'd like to think that after more than 13 years of baking, and 50+ years of 'personal experience' we've developed a unique recipe that makes every batch of our cookies and brownies something special.

I'm often asked about my background and how it is that I came to bake cookies. Like most people, my life's recipe is filled with events and experiences that, combined, brought me to where I am today. One of those experiences was meeting a man who became one of the most recognized faces on the planet based on his secret blend of 11 herbs and spices. Colonel Harlan Sanders.

I tinkered with business ideas from a very early age. In high school, I discovered an organization called Junior Achievement and that forever impacted the course of my life. Junior Achievement was an after-school program which gave me the opportunity to setup and run a real company. And to meet successful leaders and entrepreneurs like David Jones, the founder of Humana, Inc.

I had the opportunity to meet Colonel Sanders on a couple of occasions, including a brief appearance in a television commercial promoting Junior Achievement. He arrived as you might expect in his chauffeur driven white Cadillac with red leather interior, wearing his white suite and string tie. He was cordial and greeted all of us. He delivered his lines, "Your friends are in Junior Achievement. You should be too." and was driven away to his next appearance.

Later that year, I was the Master of Ceremonies for our annual banquet. We honored the Colonel for his support. During the ceremony, he stood up and handed me a personal check made out to Junior Achievement for $50,000. It left an indelible mark on my high school career, meeting someone so well-known who really cared about young people and giving back to his community.

Colonel Sanders developed and perfected his recipe for fried chicken in a small motel/restaurant, Sanders Court, in Corbin, KY. Despite the success and notoriety of the food, Interstate 75 routed traffic away from his establishment. Customers dwindled and he was forced to sell the business. At age 65, he went back out on the road, selling his franchise concept of Kentucky Fried Chicken. He had a total of $105 in his pocket.

At a time when most people are winding down their career, the Colonel was just getting started. There were many twists and turns along the road, but eventually he sold his business for $2 million, stayed on as their ambassador, and became one of the most recognized brand names in the world.

Last fall, we stopped in Corbin (as I have done in the past) to visit the original place where KFC was born. The restaurant includes areas where some of his original equipment is on display. It is a reminder and an inspiration of what can happen in business with enough persistence, patience and passion to be the best.

In addition to the Colonel's secret blend of 11 herbs and spices, his recipe for success included a strong commitment to how he treated his customers and franchise owners. The Colonel's Creed speaks volumes about what can happen when you put the right ingredients in a business, something we aspire to do at Anna's Gourmet Goodies as well. You'll find a copy of it on the wall if you happen to stop by the Cafe:

The Hard Way

> *"It is comparatively easy to prosper by trickery, the violation of confidence, of the weak….sharp practices, cutting corners – all of those methods that we are so prone to palliate and condone as "business shrewdness". It is difficult to prosper by the keeping of promises, the deliverance of value in goods, in service and in deeds – and in the meeting of so called "shrewdness" with sound merit and good ethics. The easy way is efficacious and speedy – the hard way arduous and long. But, as the clock ticks, the easy way becomes harder and the hard way becomes easier. And as the calendar records the years, it becomes increasingly evident that the easy way rests hazardously upon shifting sands, whereas the hard way builds solidly a foundation of confidence that cannot be swept away."*

While you should avoid saying 'never', it is unlikely that my face or the cookies from Anna's Gourmet Goodies will ever achieve anything close to the level of notoriety of Colonel Harlan Sanders and Kentucky Fried Chicken. I'm comfortable with that.

I do believe, however, that while there are countless places where you can purchase a cookie or a brownie made with most of the same ingredients we use (flour, butter, sugar, eggs, etc.), none will be exactly the same as what we bake at Anna's Gourmet Goodies. That's because the ingredients of a business are more than simply what is listed on the label. It contains the experiences and passions of the founders as well as the people who help run the business. A small, but important ingredient in our business came from my chance meeting with The Colonel.

What comes out of our oven every day is more than simply raw materials, it is the sum total of a lifetime of experiences and a focus on what we consider the most important measure of success for our business and what we do – to create a simple moment that brings joy and happiness to the person who bites into a cookie or brownie that we've made. It's not always been easy. Building a business takes time. But from what I learned early in life from people like the Colonel, hard work and doing the right thing is ultimately the best recipe for success.

Welcoming people at the front door

Original Post Date: April 3, 2014

The 'front door' might have changed for many businesses, but the concept still holds true - customers remember how you make them feel when they first reach out to your company. Whether it's brick and mortar or a digital door, how you greet customers sets the tone for your business.

A few weeks ago an email with a subject line, "Front Door Ideas-and a Cookie-Worth Stealing" popped into my inbox. It was a post about how a hotel chain welcomes customers at their front door with cookies (not ours – but that's okay). It made me think about some of our customers and how they use our cookies to welcome clients "at the front door". Perhaps more importantly, I thought about how we welcome clients to our front door – our website.

Making others feel welcome is something I grew up with and had the chance to share with Debbie several years ago when we visited my Aunt Opal, before she passed.

We were traveling back home and decided, on a whim, to stop by. She lived in the house where my grandmother was born in 1890, a chance to re-visit a piece of family history. We knocked on the front door for our un-announced visit (family visits in the country do not require reservations) and after exchanging greetings and hugs, we were welcomed in the house. It was close to lunchtime and she offered to prepare us a 'little something'.

I like to think that Aunt Opal was really a seven foot tall woman packed into a five foot frame. With seemingly no effort and barely taking a break from telling stories, she put together a feast that would have fed at least two dozen people. We sat down in the kitchen where my grandmother ate as a child and I can't remember a time in my life when I felt more welcome.

After lunch, we spent time catching up on family news. She gave us a tour of her garden, a plot that would have been a challenge for people half her age to tend. We left well fed, with an arm full of preserves and some rich memories. I can almost smell the cornbread and find myself re-telling this story almost fifteen years later.

What does this have to do with Anna's Gourmet Goodies? I've said this before, but it bears repeating. We bake cookies, but are really in the experience business, creating memorable impressions. To make that happen, we do our best to practice principles I learned growing up of making people feel welcome as soon as they come in the door.

This past week, we added a new client. After sending us their order, we helped them edit the message a bit, corrected a few typos (did not even tell them) and offered up an alternate package that better suited their needs and actually cost less. Yes we are happy to have the business, but more important, we wanted to make them feel comfortable and welcome right away.

When we send cookie gifts for our business clients, branded with their logo and message, we know that in many cases they are trying to make their clients feel welcome. By practicing the family values I learned growing up over and over again, we try very hard to make it look as easy as Aunt Opal did preparing that meal, leaving an equally lasting impression that hopefully will inspire recipients to tell their story to others as well.

Our 'house' might be digital (website, Facebook, Google+, Twitter), but if you happen to stop by, we'll try our best to make you feel welcome right from the start whether you are a first time customer or a member of the Anna's Gourmet Goodies family. And if we do it right, perhaps you'll tell that story to someone else 5, 10 or 20 years from now and in turn, welcome others the same way into your 'house', wherever that might be.

Sometimes a delivery failure is great service

Original Post Date: December 19, 2013

This has to be one of my favorite stories about service. In part, because of the often incorrect perception of the United States Postal Service, but also because it demonstrates what can happen when someone takes ownership and commits to being of service. It is, unfortunately, becoming rarer these days in all types of businesses. But the good news is that opens up more opportunities for those who empower and equip employees to have a service oriented mindset.

The holiday shipping season is coming to a close for us. We have cookies and brownies en route to almost every state and a couple of military bases around the world. A few of our shipments travel via FedEx, but the overwhelming majority are carried by the men and women of the United States Postal Service. While we're confident they'll arrive as scheduled, we are particularly happy that one package shipped via USPS was not delivered.

One of the things we do to make sure cookies arrive where they should is to check each address against the Postal Service database. If it doesn't return a valid 9-digit zip code, we don't ship the order. But, there are some things that we cannot catch. If it is a good address, but the recipient has moved, the package will be returned. This year we had a client call us with a different address issue that our database could not catch. It seems that the package was addressed to a husband and wife, only the wife had passed away earlier in the year and their list was simply not updated to reflect that change.

Our client called immediately once we sent the tracking information to see what could be done. I'm guessing this would not be the first time something arrived at this widower's home, but our client was genuinely concerned and asked for help.

I looked up the number for the post office in that zip code and called the Postmaster. I explained the situation, he immediately understood, and perhaps more importantly, he empathized. He asked that I send an email with the package information and a request to stop delivery. Turns out the package was actually being delivered out of another office, but he offered to handle everything. It arrived that day and was to be delivered the next morning.

I notified our customer that the Postal Service was trying to locate the package and stop delivery. I can only imagine how many packages they were processing on that day, but there was never a mention of effort required or any complaint from the Postmaster.

The next afternoon, I received a phone call. Delivery had been intercepted and the package was to be returned to Anna's Gourmet Goodies. I notified our customer and they were overwhelmed with gratitude.

Depending on who and where you strike up a conversation about the United States Postal Service, chances are good that you'll hear some type of complaint about delivery, service or whatever. Bashing the US Postal Service is right up there on some people's list with baseball, Mom and apple pie.

But it's not on my list. Frankly, we get great service from the USPS. Not perfect, but we're not either. This is one example where a delivery failure was actually the result of outstanding customer service. Not because he was required to do so, but rather because a compassionate human being understood the situation and did what he could to help. Great customer service comes from people who understand the rewards of serving others and are not afraid to take action to help.

Given the number of orders we shipped out this holiday season, odds are good that we'll get returns for some reason. And it is possible that some packages will not be delivered when they should be. Failure happens. No one on this earth is perfect. We'll do what we can to help.

You can rest assured that anytime I'm standing in a crowd and the subject of the Postal Service comes up (it does happen), you won't find me serving up any complaints. This one act of selfless service covers a lot of other mistakes. You see it just so happens that the addressee who passed away this year shares my wife's name, Debbie. And I'm very thankful that our postman won't be worried about stopping delivery of any packages coming to our home, addressed to my wife.

Real magic happens when you understand the 'why'

Original Post Date: June 28, 2013

If there is a course taught anywhere on leadership, Simon Sinek's video should be required material. In a simple yet brilliant diagram, he shows us how the most successful companies and leaders are able to create not just a following, but loyal and dedicated customers. If his work is new to you please watch his video. It just might change the way you look at your business, forever.

I was at a grand opening event not long ago when one of the hosts said to me, 'Any customer is a good customer'. It's a phrase that goes with 'The customer is always right'. Both are easy to say and sound upbeat in general conversation, but are they really true?

Don't get me wrong, we love it when customers place orders (really, don't let me stop you if you were going to click right now). The truth is, however, that not every order, or every customer, is a perfect fit for our business. I know business people who will balk at this idea and would never utter this in public. But if you've ever been so tuned in to your business that you actually 'feel the pulse', you know it is true.

Real magic in any business happens when you connect with those people who not only understand your product or service and have a need for what you provide, but who believe that you are in business for reasons that align with, and support, their values.

In a TEDx talk, Simon Sinek, diagrams what he calls the golden circle. In this circle, there are three layers, the 'what', the 'how', and the 'why'. The 'what' is on the outside, followed by the 'how'. In the center, is the 'why'.

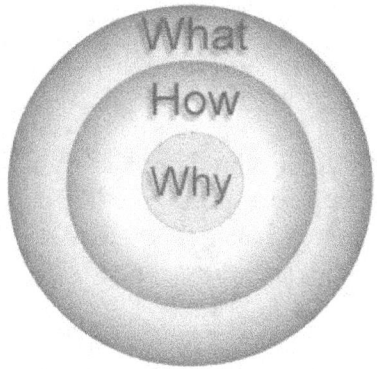

What

For Anna's Gourmet Goodies, it's pretty simple to define – we bake cookies and brownies. If this was all we focused on communicating, we would probably sell products to some customers. But, we'd be like another car horn on a busy street in Manhattan rush hour traffic vying for attention. Our cookies are good (to be sure), but there are plenty of companies out there trying to get people to buy their cookies.

How

We make our cookies by hand, using the finest ingredients. Okay. I'd hazard a guess that you'll find that phrase not just in the descriptions and brochures for other cookie businesses, but used by a slew of other companies that make food products as well. It's a process that other businesses follow. It's true, but so what.

Why

Finally, we get down to the heart of the matter. The tagline for Anna's Gourmet Goodies, 'Our cookies make people happy', describes in simple terms, why we do what we do – to bring happiness to someone's life. Sometimes it's a box of cookies (what) we ship to a client's office (how) as a thank you gift. Or it might be a gift tower (what) we send to a college student at their dorm (how) to celebrate their first birthday away from home.

In some cases, we've delivered cookies that we hope provided some measure of comfort during the last days of a person's life. All were cookies (what) that we made by hand from ingredients that we select and shipped to the end customer (how).

We believe that a simple gesture of giving someone something really good, that was lovingly made, packaged and delivered in a unique way, when they least expect it, without asking for anything in return, brings happiness and a smile to almost anyone, even if for a brief moment. It just so happens, that we also make really good cookies and brownies.

It is the why behind what we do that is the most important ingredient. We seek to deliver a brief moment of happiness to every person who opens a box of our cookies or brownies. To spark a memory. To generate a smile. To provide respite from the pressures of the day. To make people happy. That's the why.

Most businesses focus on the 'what' and the 'how'. There will always be some number of customers who order something based on answers to these questions. If anyone comes to our website, places an order with a valid credit card and address, we'll bake and ship it.

Ultimately, however, we execute on the why part of our business and attract customers who make an emotional connection to the idea of sharing happiness by sending one of our gifts to another person. They value what we do beyond simply the amount of money spent on a purchase.

Fortunately, the world of technology we live in today has made finding the why easier than ever. We can search, post, share, like and collaborate with our friends next door and around the globe, all at the click of a button. The war for transparency in business is over – the Internet won.

What might happen in your business or your life if you were to stop and focus on the why? Would it make a difference in the customers you attract or the people in your life? I believe that it does. And once you've had a taste of that magic (sort of like our chocolate chip cookies), nothing else tastes quite as sweet.

If you should decide to send a gift to someone, or maybe you have opened a box of our cookies with a cold glass of milk at some time, I want you to know that the why will always be the same – to make people happy.

The business benefits of pruning blueberry bushes

Original Post Date: October 30, 2012

The most common form of pruning in business almost always makes the news - layoffs. There's no doubt that this has a negative impact on those affected, especially in the short term. During the dotcom bust in the early 2000's, I had the opportunity to witness it firsthand. But there are other types of pruning businesses can perform, some of which might just help reduce or eliminate the major limb cutting that usually comes as a last resort.

I can't remember exactly when the blueberry bushes at my family's camp on the banks of the Pungo Creek in Eastern NC grew out of control, but they most certainly did. Despite suffering from several years of neglect, they produced an abundant crop of fruit. But the bushes had become trees, the neighboring scuppernong vines were invading their branches and other foliage including briers and the infectious mimosa were taking root among them. It was a sight that as a neighbor pointed out to me one day, would have caused the late Dr. Susan Dees, or Grampy as we called her, to throw a 'hissy fit'.

It might not seem obvious at first, but you can learn a lesson about running a business by pruning blueberry bushes.

About three years ago I made it my personal mission to pay proper attention to these plants and restore them to their glory. Despite the fact that Dr. Dees left us more than 10 years ago, I can't help but feel her presence whenever I'm down there. Having a proper chore to balance out the lazy afternoon in the hammock has always been the price of a weekend in my NC paradise. Adopting the blueberry and scuppernong vines seemed only fitting and has proven to be both therapeutic and educational.

You might think that trimming blueberries, running a business and baking cookies are totally unrelated, but like most things I enjoy, I try to learn and draw comparisons whenever I can. You see, a business is not unlike a plant. With water, sun and soil, it grows. It produces fruit. You collect the harvest. And you try to keep the cycle going.

Businesses, like plants, need attention and require occasional pruning to grow as they were intended. This does not mean that if you leave a business alone, it will stop growing. That does happen, but some businesses grow well without much oversight at all. They sometimes become wild patches of things that bear fruit and have little resemblance to their original form. Sometimes this is good. Sometimes, it is not.

If you let them go long enough, well, they might just grow into something they are not intended to be and eventually, die. If you let blueberry bushes go too long without a good trimming, they turn into trees. When the trees get too tall and the fruit too heavy, the branches bend down to the ground. Eventually, they grow sideways, break or simply die.

The problem I faced in pruning the bushes came down to one thing, plain and simple – fear. They clearly needed a serious cleaning, but cut too much and they might not recover. After all, they'd been producing blueberries for probably 40 years or more. Replanting them was possible, but replacing their history was not.

I believe this happens sometimes in businesses. We get used to doing things and as long as the products are selling and money keeps coming in, we focus on the fruit, not necessarily the health of the whole business. It is difficult to prune products and especially, customers. But just like the scuppernong vines choking the blueberry bushes and the mimosa trees growing in their midst, businesses take on products or customers that are not the best fit and can eventually choke out even a healthy, profitable business.

We originally incorporated our company late in 2001 and began selling pies and cakes in 2002. We changed over to cookies beginning in 2004 and have had a few product ideas come and go over the years. The wholesale dessert business became less and less a good fit for our operation as the cookie business began to grow and thrive. Just like scuppernong grapes, making and selling wholesale desserts is not a bad business by itself, just not the best fit for how the business at Anna's Gourmet Goodies was developing.

Pruning that part of the business was scary, much like those first cuts I made on the blueberry bushes. But, we did so thoughtfully, a little at a time. Like an artist painting on a big canvas, you cut a little, step back, take a look and then cut a little more. Everyone has their own style and while I'm sure there are plenty of people who would come in with a chainsaw and clear everything in a few hours, I prefer to prune slowly and intentionally.

A few weeks ago marked the one year anniversary since we pruned the last branch from the tree of our wholesale dessert business. I delivered the last Chocolate Oatmeal Pie to our longtime friend Judy Wishart at the Olde English Tea Room in downtown Wake Forest. It was scary to let go of the very part of our business that was the foundation of the company. But just like the blueberry bushes, it was time to trim this part of the business. What would happen? Would we die? Or continue to grow?

If you've had the opportunity to hear me speak on what it's like to own a business, you know that I'm a big believer in using your own yardstick to measure success. Top line, bottom line, social impact, peace of mind, family values – they are all important measurements that vary from person to person and no single measurement is right for everyone.

I honestly don't watch numbers at Anna's Gourmet Goodies nearly as close as I watch cookies and the quality of what we do, but I can tell you our sales are up nicely over the same period for 2011. This holiday season is still a large variable, but the pruning we did in 2011 has turned out okay, so far.

I was back down to the Pungo Creek last weekend and gave the bushes a serious haircut, more than in years past. It was a bit scary, but I trust that my years of patience will be fruitful. I won't know for sure until sometime next summer. I'll just have to wait and have faith that I've pruned the right amount.

We're heading into the busy season for Anna's Gourmet Goodies. We've watched some of our customers go by the wayside, while we are enjoying connecting and meeting new folks who've discovered our website and find it refreshingly clean and easy to navigate. I'll be doing a bit more pruning and preparation before the holiday season and while I might not know the exact outcome for some time, I'll have faith that time spent tending and pruning this business will help us bear good fruit, or in our case, a whole lot of cookies and brownies over the next few months. Only time will tell.

Have you checked your company's cholesterol?

Original Post Date: January 14, 2009

Every company has some measurement to evaluate their health. In today's world of analytics and 'big data', there are probably more ways and things to measure than we have people to evaluate. It's worth taking time to step back and look beyond the obvious or common logic, to discover underlying elements of the business that might be the ultimate cause of problems down the road. Sometimes these little things are not that obvious, but could make a huge impact.

I'm not great with New Year's Resolutions, but I do like to be reflective this time of year and try to think about what I have learned, how I can improve, and whether or not I need to adjust my sails. Earlier this past summer, my wife and I went in for our every other year annual physical and it turned out to be a learning experience. While regular checkups are a good idea, we are incredibly healthy and just don't make many visits to our friendly family doctor.

This year, our doctor suggested we include a new blood test from a local company, Liposcience. It's called an NMR LipoProfile test. I have some family history of heart disease and this is a new way to look at one of the culprits, cholesterol. My first reaction was to pass on the test, especially given that my levels have always bordered on being too low – with my last check being somewhere in the 120 range. Not bad for someone that bakes cookies with butter for a living. (FYI – my grandparents ate fried pork, eggs, and biscuits with redeye gravy at LEAST once a day and lived to be 86 – go figure).

But our doctor is very well read and a great guy who is not into the latest 'pharma fad', so I opted to give them an extra vile of my blood to check. The theory behind this test is that it is not necessarily the level of cholesterol that really matters. But rather, it is the number and size of the lipoprotein particles that carry the cholesterol in my bloodstream that are the real determinate of whether or not I am at risk for developing plaque in my arteries.

He explained that the interior walls of the artery are not really solid, but have small pockets or holes that allow molecules to pass through. Their theory, and it seemed logical, is that if there are a large number of small particles carrying the cholesterol, they can easily become lodged in these openings, building up, and eventually leading to hardening of the arteries, blockage, and all the ugliness that comes along with stoppage of blood flow to the heart.

When Debbie went for her physical a few weeks later, she also opted for the test. We were anxious to get the results, given that her cholesterol level has always been on the high side, north of 200, long before we ever started the cookie business. Would the test results shed any new light on our health profiles?

I received my lab results back first and it was indeed a surprise and right in line with Doc's thinking. My cholesterol, although very low (<150), was being carried in a high number of small particles, putting me in a higher risk category. I'm not sedentary, have been practicing yoga three times a week for the past 6 years and am well within my weight range. No pills or diets, just a life of moderation. Debbie's results came in shortly thereafter and sure enough, her cholesterol level was above 'normal'. However, the LipoProfile showed her particles were fewer and very large, putting her in the lowest risk category. This is exactly the opposite of what traditional thinking might render. If you've stayed with me this far, you must be wondering 'What in the world does this have to do with business?'

As we just put to rest what will most likely be recorded as one of the most disastrous years for the economy in my lifetime, I've been thinking about what really lead us up to these seemingly unfathomable problems. After all, just a few years ago we were ticking along nicely, knowing that we are always prone to economic cycles, but not fearing death of the likes of American Home Mortgage, Lehman Brothers, Wachovia and others. I'm thinking we might want to examine the patient from a new perspective, challenging the 'traditional thinking' of what causes these types of major problems. Perhaps we should be looking at the quantity of small, almost microscopic problems that have become so systemic in business today, as the real killer.

Maybe these silent, almost imperceptible issues that go on every day in all types of operations are the catalyst that eventually leads to this type of economic myocardial infarction. Risk may very well come, not from the big problems that everyone sees and talks about, but rather from these smaller issues that embed themselves slowly over time, leading to serious and sometimes fatal consequences for a business.

I'm certain that virtually every one reading this post can recant stories from your workplace or other businesses, where issues were ignored, overlooked or just plain dismissed as not that important. It goes on every day, in small and medium businesses and especially in the larger companies where operational and ethical problems are easy to hide. Earlier this spring, Debbie and I strolled in to our local bank branch to refinance our home equity line of credit and lower the interest rate. We had not been in the branch much before and had never met the loan officer. We walked in, introduced ourselves, sat down, signed the paperwork that was already prepared and re-indebted ourselves. When we finished the transaction, I asked the loan officer why she never asked for any ID. How did she know it was really us? We never provided any proof of ID, income, address, or anything.

In our case, this was clearly a legitimate transaction, but I'm wondering how many times over the past years these transactions happened where perhaps things were not in order. At banks, at insurance companies, car manufacturers, technology companies – the list goes on and on. Business now moves almost at the speed of thought, and it might be that very thing that has helped put us at risk for serious problems. By moving too quickly, businesses and ultimately the people that run them, ignore the details, allow decisions to be made that are not right, but easy to let go, and create what will ultimately be fatal outcomes for many institutions in our economy.

"So Doc, how do I fix this small molecule problem?" Fortunately, it was a fairly simple solution. I need more aerobic exercise and to increase my intake of omega-3 fats. So I'm back on the fish oil pills with a vengeance. And, while it has taken some effort to consistently roll out of bed and hop on the bike for my morning ride, it has given me a fresh perspective on life and business. I'm afraid the solution for businesses and our economy might not be that simple.

To begin with, you have to recognize the problem and I fear that our leaders, execs and many individuals are still too busy pointing fingers instead of getting to the root of the disease. Despite the wave of 'change' that has swept through our electoral offices this past November, I'm not convinced the bureaucrats understand the problem, the intricacies of running a business, or how to craft a real solution. There is no simple fix, but here are a couple of ideas that might help:

- **Embrace creative thought.** If you have ever worked in, or created an environment where, creative thinking is squelched, then you've been in a business with carotid arteries. The flow of ideas is the lifeblood of business. Ask more questions. Eliminate 'No' as a first response. Put on a different pair of eyes. Avoid complacency. You never really know where the solution to a problem or the next million dollar idea is going to come from.

- **Think it through.** I have a copy of 'Don't Sweat the Small Stuff' on my bookshelf and understand the pain of micro-management, but I believe it is critical to examine processes, decisions and actions in detail. Think through the ramifications. Small issues and problems can be cumulative and have catastrophic consequences. Take responsibility. Take time. And as Thomas Watson said, 'THINK'.

- **Do the right thing.** Early this past fall, I went back to my alma mater, The Fuqua School of Business, to facilitate a day of reflection for the returning students on their summer work experience. The focus of the event was to talk about decision making and courage in the workplace. The courage to do the right thing in what professor Joe Leboeuf called, 'moments that matter – when no one is looking'. Stop protecting your ego. Remember the Golden Rule. When you do the right thing consistently, you develop mental toughness and set a benchmark that helps keep your life, your career and your business healthy.

Focusing on small problems might be a hard sell for those who only look at the world from the thirty thousand foot level, but Doc has me sold. So I'll be cycling down the road, swallowing a fish oil pill, and thinking about managing my life and my businesses so that I avoid what Fred Sanford comically referred to as 'The Big One'. It might be too late for Lehman and many others, but there are plenty of businesses out there that might want to get a thorough physical, change perspective on sweating the details and come out for a ride.

Could Lagniappe be a Solution?

Original Post Date: November 15, 2008

Outside of a few friends from New Orleans, I have not met a single person who could tell me what this word means, much less pronounce it. And yet, when you understand the concept and think about how it relates to business and the relationship with customers, it has the potential to impact the entire culture of a company, for the better.

Last year about this time, a customer and friend, Renee from Uptown Endodontics in New Orleans, introduced me to a new word that has become one of my favorites when I think about Anna's Gourmet Goodies and our business, 'lagniappe' (pronounced lan-yap). It's Cajun and means, 'a little something extra'. When we filled one of her large orders last year for their clients, we sent her the same basket to try. No charge – just a little something extra. She thanked us for the lagniappe.

We actually love to do this with clients throughout the year. We sometimes send out thank you gifts to our clients in August, at a time when most folks least expect them. And we've been known to 'accidentally drop' a few extra packs of cookies in someone's order. It is such a great feeling to do something nice for someone when they are not expecting it.

One of my favorite restaurants in Raleigh is The Duck and the Dumpling. Chef David Mao has been a long time customer of ours and if you have the chance to dine there you might just find lagniappe in the form of his delicious carrot ginger soup, or some other culinary surprise before or after your meal.

When I step back a few feet and look at our business, that's really what Anna's Gourmet Goodies is all about – doing something nice for someone when they are not expecting it. It's an attitude with which we approach our business and our life. Some of our most successful clients in the automobile, insurance, mortgage, financial services and other industries have embraced this philosophy and made it a part of their business. One of our customers that sends cookies to their employees as birthday gifts and has them delivered to the office on Saturday mornings, recently surveyed their staff about what they liked most about the company and you guessed it, our cookies ranked up there in the top five. Small gesture – big impact.

I've been thinking about this lately, especially in light of all the negativity of the elections and the economic implosion that dominates virtually every major media outlet. It seems that all we hear about is 'cutting back'. There is no doubt in my mind that we are in this mess because of greed and excess at all levels of government, business and individual lifestyles, and a little trimming is in order. The focus on 'what's in it for me' as opposed to 'what can I do for someone else' has definitely tipped the scales to the former.

However, could lagniappe be a solution to some of the economic and societal challenges we face? Maybe. I guess it depends, like most anything, on how it is used. From my perspective lagniappe doesn't mean thinking that if I just put this extra package of cookies in a box, that I immediately expect something in return. It's not about spending big bucks to impress or bribe people. It's about doing something nice that brings a smile to someone's face, to make them feel good – just because. If this sounds a little sappy, stop and think about the last time someone did a little something extra for you and how it made you feel about them and/or the company. Talk about making your business stand out in a crowd – it's really a 'no-brainer'.

When I see people and companies trying to 'dig their way out' of a hole, I'm wondering if the real solution is to stop digging and focus on what you can do to help someone else. In return, you'll find it easier to take a step up and climb out, when someone inevitably reaches out their hand in turn, to help you.

We're about to enter the season of the year when Anna's Gourmet Goodies will be busy sending gifts for companies and individuals. I've been getting questions from people who pay too much attention to the news, about our business and whether we see everyone cutting back. While we have had a few companies decide to forgo what they consider to be the 'extras', I'm also finding just as many new folks that understand the value of lagniappe, calling us with their holiday gift orders. I am certain that at the end of this storm these individuals and companies will be standing on top of the sand dune, rather than being buried with those who focused totally on 'hunkering down' to wait it out.

I know Renee will understand that while I truly appreciate their business, I am hopefully not in the market any time soon for any endodontic (aka root canal) work. But if I were, it might just be worth a trip down to The Big Easy. I'm absolutely confident that in addition to superior service and a comfortable procedure, there would be lagniappe just for being a patient. And of course, I'd bring along a pocket full of cookies.

Charity

"Where there is charity and wisdom, there is neither fear nor ignorance."

- Saint Francis of Assisi

The ripple effect of kindness

Original Post Date: February 16, 2017

Have you ever noticed that when you witness an act of kindness, you feel better? Studies now indicate that simply witnessing an act of kindness releases serotonin in our brain. One way to keep this flowing is to participate in acts of kindness. Again, studies show that acts of kindness have tremendous health benefits. Even simple acts offer big rewards. Give it a try.

One of my favorite memories from childhood is skipping rocks at our family's house on Nolin Lake. Some mornings, when the water was still like a piece of glass, with a hint of fog rising just above the surface, we'd skip rocks and watch the ripples gently spread across the silvery surface, eventually joining together and fading in the distance. I was reminded of this recently after watching a simple act of kindness and experiencing the ripple effect of that act for myself.

Early in the morning on one of my long walks through the historic district of Wake Forest I noticed my friend Durward Matheny in the distance. His office is in the Wake Forest Museum property and I commonly see him out and about, even on a Saturday morning. He stopped his car in front of a B&B that just sold after the owner's husband died. He picked up the newspaper off the front lawn, carefully put in on the front porch, and walked back to his car.

It was a simple act of kindness, done without any thought of repayment or acknowledgment. Having known Durward for more than 20 years, it is not the least bit surprising he would do something like this, but it struck me at that moment just how important even the smallest of gestures can be. I had not spoken with him recently and struck up a conversation. He told me he was speaking at a fundraiser for the Koinonia Foundation later that day. They were having a silent auction and dinner to raise money.

After catching up, I continued my walk, determined to continue the 'ripple of kindness' I saw in Durward that morning. I went back to the bakery, put together a tin of cookies and brownies and dropped it by the location where the auction was to be held that evening. No paperwork. No receipt. I just wanted to create a ripple that ultimately would benefit someone less fortunate and blessed than I am.

A few days later, as Valentine's Day rolled around I found an opportunity to create yet another ripple. Anna asked me to sell a very large stuffed bear (almost 4' tall) she received as a Valentine's present that no longer held any meaning for her. Instead of selling the bear, we picked up a bucket, baked up a batch of cookies, added some balloons and dropped off both at Duke Cancer Center Raleigh.

I met Kim, one of the nurses there, and explained that we simply wanted to offer up cookies to the nurses and patients in the chemo ward, spreading a little love on Valentine's Day. I also wanted some patient in need of a little kindness, to take home the bear. She immediately understood my intent and with a big smile on her face, proceeded to take the cookies and the bear off to create yet another ripple.

The lady at the gift shop smiled as I was leaving and told me that it was a 'sweet gesture'. I explained how the nurses and staff had done such an amazing job taking care of Dawn, one of our 'cookie helpers' during her chemo therapy. Fighting back the tears, I let her know that it was me who received the gift that day.

I share stories like this with our friends at Anna's Gourmet Goodies in hopes that it will inspire even one person, in some way. We're in the gift business, creating memories for those recipients who enjoy our cookies and brownies. But over the years I've found that when it comes to giving back, I'm the one who actually receives the gift of being able to make a ripple every now and then.

I can't remember a time in our nation's history when we are in need of more 'ripples of kindness'. If you agree, here's a recipe that might help:

Step one: Take a break from the news

Step two: Stop complaining about or talking about supporting/not supporting anything

Step three: Find someone who is in need and do something to help, even if it's as simple as picking up the paper and putting it on their porch.

I'll never know where the money from the silent auction goes or who got the bear. But just like skipping rocks at Nolin Lake on one of those cool mornings, I'm pretty sure I created a small ripple. Imagine what might happen if more and more people started creating ripples of kindness.

In the meantime, we'll be baking up cookies and sending them out to people for their birthday, as a thank you gift or as we did on Valentine's Day, to a student away at school as a reminder that Mom and Dad love him very much. If there's someone in your company or personal life that might benefit from a little recognition, please visit our website and let us know how we can help. We promise to take special care of every package that goes out of our bakery and to help you create a ripple of kindness whenever possible.

One doesn't have to be the loneliest number

Original Post Date: November 4, 2015

There are so many great charities that support women diagnosed with breast cancer that it can be difficult to choose. I've supported several over the years, but found this one to be especially compelling as they help women with the basic necessities that are required for everyday life after diagnosis. And, the name is a powerful reminder of just how prevalent this disease is today - affecting more than 10 percent of the female population. If you don't know someone yet, chances are you will.

I shared the 'Starfish Story' in an earlier post and I was touched by the number of people who reached out to let me know how much they enjoyed the story. It's about making a difference, one act at a time.

It's pretty easy these days to take a look around your neighborhood or the world and be overwhelmed by the number of people in need. Instead of throwing in the towel, I remind myself that one gesture matters.

At Anna's Gourmet Goodies, we regularly receive requests for donations for a range of organizations, especially during this time of year. Some we've supported in the past, and some find us through Internet search. And while we simply can't say yes to every request, it is something we genuinely enjoy doing.

October was Breast Cancer Awareness month for 2015. In the US, about 1 in 8 women will develop invasive breast cancer over the course of her lifetime. (Let that sink in for a minute...) With numbers that high, it is not surprising to see so many organizations working to take on this insidious disease. While that can be a good thing, the sheer magnitude of the problem can be a little overwhelming.

This year nearly a quarter of a million women will be diagnosed with invasive breast cancer.

We're fortunate to have an organization in our area focused on making a difference for some of these women, one at a time. 1in9 is an organization whose ultimate goal is to ease some of the burdens that come along with the diagnosis of breast cancer. These might be emotional, physical or financial. They seek to make sure that women who find themselves to be the one in nine (or eight) don't make that journey alone.

On November 14, 2015, they'll be holding their annual fundraiser, A Pink Tie Affair at the Masquerade Ball. We'll be providing cookies for the sponsor and guest tables along with items for their auction. Specifically, donors will have the chance to bid on certificates to send a gift from Anna's Gourmet Goodies as a part of the initial care package women accepted into 1in9 receive.

Find your one

If giving back is something you've incorporated into your business and/or your life, congrats and keep on keepin' on. If not, I'd encourage you to find the one starfish you can help with your time, talents and/or treasure. Turns out my Mom's advice was once again, spot on. It's not gift, but the thought that counts.

One more thing

There's one more reason why I'm giving back to 1in9 this year. Last October my wife Debbie received a phone call from the radiology group asking her to come back for a second mammogram. She was not nearly as worried as I was, writing it off as one of those things that happens sometimes.

After the second mammogram, the doctor went back thru all her records for the past 10 years and determined that indeed, something showed up that did not look right. They wanted to go in and do a biopsy.

The few hours we spent in the doctor's office that day went by in slow motion, each minute felt like a day. It was obvious that the staff at the reception desk had experience and training managing anxious husbands. Maybe the cookie samples helped a little. I can't say for sure.

The next few days waiting for the results felt like years. It all happened so fast, but seemed to take forever. The procedure was on a Friday and I'm certain it was the longest weekend of my life.

Finally we got the call to come in for the results. When the doctor opened the door to the room and came in, I could see from the smile on her face that we were indeed blessed that Debbie was not going to be one of the nine women on this day.

This year it's estimated that nearly a quarter of a million women will not be as lucky as Debbie. They'll be diagnosed with invasive breast cancer and begin a new chapter in their life. And for at least a few of those women, we'll have the honor of sending a small package, filled with cookies and love that hopefully, will make the first few steps of this walk just a little bit easier, and not quite so lonely.

P.S. If you don't have an organization like 1in9 in your community and are moved to help in some way, learn more by visiting their website 1in9.com.

Real miracles happen daily in this place

Original Post Date: September 25, 2013

Besides the health benefits of doing volunteer work and benefits to the receiving organization, I've found another benefit - perspective. As the pace of life and work accelerates, our perspective tends to become more narrow as we focus on getting tasks done, making it through the day. Just as you cannot safely drive by constantly looking down at the road, we need to step back, look around, find our place on a map, and get a little perspective.

Earlier this past summer, we challenged Anna to come up with some 'mission projects' centered around community service. She spent the last year in the YMCA Leader's Club, where she had to spend at least 10 hours a month volunteering. To reinforce what she was learning, I offered up resources at Anna's Gourmet Goodies to help with the project(s) she put together.

Scan back through my blog, you'll find a post about the Ronald McDonald House in Durham (RMHD), and my last one about 'The Why'. If you combine those two, you'll understand why serving dinner for guests at RMHD seemed like the perfect combination for one of Anna's mission projects.

We wanted to make a dinner that everyone would enjoy, but also create an experience that was special. Pasta is a common dinner, but we decided to make it fresh, on site, using a hand crank pasta maker.

And rather than sauce from a jar, we opted for fresh marinara starting with real tomatoes, carrots, onions and fresh herbs from our garden. We added a salad of organic greens and spinach, along with loaves of organic whole wheat baguettes from our friends at Whole Foods Market, and kicked it up a notch with a roasted garlic and butter sauce. And of course, we baked up a fresh batch of our 'magic cookies' to finish things off.

RMHD recently expanded and has the capacity to house up to 55 families at a time. For our meal, we were told to plan on feeding about 75 people. That's a lot of handmade pasta, so we enlisted the help of two of Anna's friends, Elise and Oliva.

After a busy day in our kitchen getting as much prepared as possible, we headed out for Durham to start cooking in their spacious state of the art common area kitchen. We wanted to make sure the guests enjoyed a memorable meal, prepared from scratch with extra love and care.

We had the chance to meet and talk with several of the guests while preparing the meal. Fresh pasta is a real treat to eat as well as watching it being made. It was fun getting to know the families while we were busy cranking, stirring and preparing the meal. We met one family who was spending their last evening at RMHD, returning the next day to Bethel, Alaska. Her daughter had come to Duke for ear surgery and they spent about three months at the house. I tried to calculate the distance from Durham to Bethel, but Google maps simply could not return the calculation – rest assured it is a long way from their home.

The dinner rush came at 6:30 when they announced our menu to the house. We helped guests, some weary from a long day at the hospital, navigate the buffet line and made sure everyone was served.

When we were almost ready to close up, a husband and wife came down with their daughter for dinner. While the father attended to the daughter, the mother filled up her plate. She was happy, smiling, and very grateful, so I struck up a conversation by asking about her stay at RMHD. She explained the details of her newborn baby's condition and the challenges she faced. I listened intently as she described how doctors were working to correct something never before seen in medical history.

It seems that her internal organs where not developed and she would undergo multiple surgeries to have any hope of correcting the problem. That day, the newborn was fighting an infection from the last surgery. If everything went well, she said they might return home for Christmas.

She went on to explain that as a child, she too faced serious health challenges and was herself a patient at Duke Children's Hospital. The entire time we spoke, she had a smile on her face and seemed genuinely happy. I held back tears and was both honored and humbled by her story.

I wish that I could tell you that our cookies (and the rest of our meal) somehow contributed to her happiness, but that would simply not be true. Her happiness came from her faith and gratitude – plain and simple. This was one case where I was actually the recipient of her happiness, not the other way around.

After the last guest was served, we cleaned up the kitchen and put away the food. We left behind a couple of cookies and some leftover pasta, but I suspect that it disappeared by the next day.

I've thought about this experience over the past weeks and wanted to share a couple of thoughts. First of all, I am grateful to our customers. Without your support over the years, it would not be possible for us to do even small projects like this one, and give something back to our community.

Secondly, it reinforces the rewards of being of service to others. Of doing something, whether it is making cookies, preparing a meal, lending a hand or sometimes your ear, to bring a brief moment of happiness to someone else.

And finally, it serves as another reminder of the importance of perspective. We are fortunate that Anna's Gourmet Goodies has been growing this past year, but like any business, we'll face challenges and obstacles in the coming months and years. But probably none as great as that young baby lying in a bed at Duke Children's Hospital, waiting for the skill of the surgeon's hands to give her the opportunity to live life itself. In comparison, I have no problems.

RMHD sent us a nice thank you note after the dinner, but it was really us who should be thanking them. My friend and the director Oie Osterkamp told me that one of the board members suggested that the letters RMHD really stand for 'Real Miracles Happen Daily'. After spending a little time there, meeting the guests, and hearing their stories, I'd have to agree. I'm just grateful for the opportunity to come along for the ride.

Give without expectation and it comes back

Original Post Date: July 14, 2011

I find that giving is sort of like a boomerang, except that it seems to work best when I toss it, not expecting it to return. It's not always immediate, but without fail, it seems that eventually it returns to me. Not always in proportion, sometimes less and sometimes more. And even when it does not return, the gift of giving, as we learned in an earlier post, has benefits for the giver as well as the recipient.

As a gourmet cookie company, we certainly get our share of requests for donations. We try our best to balance the needs of the business while giving back to the community. One of our favorite groups to support is the NC Special Olympics. We've been providing cookies to fuel these athletes for the past several years. Bill and Darlene McKenney are friends and members of the Wake Forest Civitan Club. Members of the club volunteer and serve lunch to the athletes.

This year, we added labels to the cookie packages with a few words of encouragement to support their quest to give their best effort. In addition to a great cookie, we wanted to add a little extra to help put a smile on 600 or so faces when they are giving it their all.

I received another request today from an organization, and while it might be a worthwhile event, I decided to pass. They asked for free cookies as gifts and prizes for a member reception. In exchange for the gift, I was to get my name in front of 100 or so 'potential customers'.

I'm certain that I've lost out on plenty of promotional opportunities in the past, but that's not the primary reason we donate. Supporting a group just to (hopefully) make a profit sometime in the future is simply not my style. I like to think we put our support to work where it can really make a difference.

That's not to say I don't get repaid many times over when we give. It just seems to come back to me when I least expect it. A surprise. A small measure of gratitude. A sign post that lets me know I'm on the right path. Last week, it came from Tim Minard, a hot dog vendor at Waterfront Park in Louisville, KY.

We ventured back to Kentucky for a weekend wedding. We spent a day driving around Louisville and decided to take my two Anna's (that's another story) down to the Waterfront Park on the Ohio River. The river is not for swimming, but it did not take the girls long to find water spouts to take the edge off the 95 plus degree heat.

We were walking around and Debbie left her purse in the car. She is the keeper of cash in our family. The girls asked for some water so I strolled over to the hot dog stand to see what I could find.

I asked if they accepted credit cards. "No, I'm sorry we don't. What did you need?" I explained that I was looking for some water for my daughter and niece, but had only plastic for payment. He pulled out a couple of bottles and handed them to me before I could say no. "No charge" he said.

I noticed he was wearing a visor with the Special Olympics logo on it. Turns out that Tim is a big supporter of Special Olympics and recently helped raise more than $70,000. His company, Dogs on the Run, works with Special Olympics Indiana for Area 2. I could tell by the look in his eyes that he understood what it means to give something back with no expectation of a return. Just because it is the right thing to do.

It was not until after he gave me the water that I shared my story of donating cookies for the athletes. Maybe it was pure coincidence, but I said a quiet 'thank you', smiled and enjoyed a conversation with a new found friend.

If you happen to be in Louisville, I'd recommend you get off on River Road and look for the Dogs on the Run cart. Tim will serve up a fine dog, a cold drink and a friendly smile. And you can be sure that some small measure of what you spend will help an athlete you'll never meet at next year's Special Olympics. You can smile knowing that you made a difference in the life of someone out there giving their best effort. In my book, that's what it means to give something back.

Sowing seeds of hope

Original Post Date: January 29, 2010

It can be overwhelming. When you stop to look at all the needs in the world today, which is easy to do thanks to social media, it is easy to freeze like a deer in the headlights. Unless you have significant financial resources, how do you begin to make an impact? When you give or volunteer from the heart, you are sowing seeds that may turn into a significant harvest one day. Think small. Do something. Repeat.

Try as I may, I simply cannot imagine what it must have been like. I've been without a home before, but I always found shelter. We lived through hurricane Fran in 1996 and were without power, but still had food, clean clothes and water. For those mothers, fathers, brothers, sisters, sons and daughters half a world away in the tiny nation of Haiti, they watched everything they know disappear in a matter of seconds. No warning. The earth shook. Buildings crumbled. People died. And life as they know it was changed, forever.

I say it often, and events like this bring it into sharp focus, that we are indeed blessed with a life far more abundant than we stop to appreciate. Tony Robbins once said in a story about a family losing a loved one suddenly in a violent act, that 'We have no problems. That family has problems.' I think the same can be said about us when thinking of the people of Haiti, we have no problems.

Hardly a day goes by when I do not see someone, somewhere, in need. Feeling as though I can't help them all, I often freeze and end up not doing anything. But I was moved by the magnitude of this event and decided to take action and offer up a little seed of hope to people I will certainly never meet.

The owners of a local restaurant felt the same and decided to enable folks like myself to do something to help. Joe Lumbrazo, owner of The Backyard Bistro located behind the RBC Center in Raleigh, teamed up with Sean Bunn and The Triangle Red Sox Nation fan club to put together a relief effort. They agreed to rent a trailer, cook up some spectacular BBQ, and invite folks in the community to come and donate clothing and other items. They furnished the collection vehicle, the logistics, and the food — all we had to do was help fill it up.

I seek out learning opportunities for my daughter and we've been trying to help Anna understand just what it might be like for the people of Haiti. Imagine that one minute you are standing in the living room, and the next minute you are covered with walls, and boards, and shingles. You claw your way out from under what once was your home. You hear people screaming and crying. And there is silence. You look for Mom and Dad, but you cannot find them. They could be alive, but they could also be dead. There are neighbors around. Many are injured and bleeding. Some are searching for their family. Everything you own is now sitting in a crumbled pile of debris. You sit on the ground. No food. No water. Only tears to wet your face.

This past holiday season, Anna's Gourmet Goodies ended up with an extra case of cookie tins that we could not sell. So, we decided to assemble some personal hygiene kits for the people of Haiti. Anna and I headed off to the store to pick up some wash cloths, soap, toothpaste and a toothbrush. We put everything neatly into the tins, included a prayer, a note of encouragement, and tied them up with a blue ribbon.

In addition to the kits, Anna and I also cleaned out our clothes closet, making a conscious effort to select not just things that are old and worn out, but nice things that I still wear, but can do without. We loaded up the back of the car and headed out to The Backyard Bistro.

We arrived a little more than an hour after the event started, and the trailer was already near half full. The BBQ was excellent, and it felt great to meet and greet other people that were sowing their seeds of hope as well. A van from a local church arrived just as we were leaving, filled with gifts and warm smiles for the people of Haiti. While we did not stay until the event ended at 3:00 p.m., I understand that they collected enough to fill half of a semi-tractor trailer in about four hours. Since then, more has come in.

I came back home that afternoon and celebrated a milestone birthday with my family, a few friends and some neighbors. We swapped stories, snacked and enjoyed a Pear and Chocolate cake that Debbie made along with some ice cream. She set the whole thing up and asked that people bring food to share in lieu of any gifts. As it turns out, planting a few seeds of hope in the back of a trailer bound for Haiti might just be one of the best birthday gifts I've ever received. It's certainly one I'll remember for some time to come.

And while our contribution might have been small in comparison to the recent telethon effort, you just never know how something so small might grow. Have you looked at a mustard seed lately? Find something that moves you and toss out a few seeds of hope. Sometimes, even a small seed can make a big difference.

Thoughts

"When you change the way you see things, the things you see will change."

- Dr. Wayne Dyer

A great harvest takes time and work

Original Post Date: July 9, 2014

We want it and want it now. Need an answer, ask Google. Need groceries, clothing or whatever - order online and have it delivered, sometimes within hours. The quantum transformation in technology has conditioned us to believe that we can have everything, right now. While that is true and beneficial in some areas of life and work, some things still take time to nurture before we reap the reward.

Sometimes in our personal lives and our work (yes – even in the cookie business), we do things that need to be done, with no immediately visible benefit or payoff. In the digital world, we have near instant feedback, access to information, friends, family, resources and more. There are however, worthwhile things we must do that require time and effort without immediate feedback or reward.

In October 2012, I wrote a post titled 'The business benefits of pruning blueberry bushes". (If you were not among the two or three people who read it, you can check it out here.) It was another of my attempts to draw lessons from seemingly unrelated life activities. Pruning is one of those things that farmers and gardeners know is essential for plants and trees, but it has many parallels to life and business as well.

About five years ago I decided to take on the task of reviving the blueberry bushes at our family's camp near on the Pungo Creek in eastern North Carolina. They had suffered from years of neglect and were over grown with other vegetation. I worked in the early fall and late winter by removing what did not look right – other trees and plants that had claimed space among the blueberries. Thorny vines strangled the bushes, preventing them from bearing the wonderful fruit they were intended to produce. It was real work cleaning out all the unwanted plants and trees and transferring them to the burn pile, but a welcome respite from the mental stress of running a business.

I felt the work had value, but knew it would not produce any immediate results. It might be years before I saw the result of my efforts. Knowing that if I cut too deeply, they might not survive, I took the longer view, doing a little bit of work each season. We visited some during the summer months in the years following and I watched as the bushes began to recover, yielding some fruit each year.

During this time, we also did some cleaning and pruning at Anna's Gourmet Goodies, balancing the need to remove activities that would allow us to grow without damaging the core business. It was hard, especially after the downturn of 2007-2008, but we continued to make changes that felt right and would hopefully yield a harvest over the long term.

That process continued over the past several years and I extended it to other areas as well. Earlier in 2014, I 'pruned' another business interest where I had invested significant time, effort and resources. Not an easy thing, but it felt like the right thing to do, giving me more room to grow in the long term.

During these past five years, an interesting thing happened at Anna's Gourmet Goodies. When we stop and look back at the results, an area of our business that we wanted to grow, managing birthday and anniversary gifts, has begun to flourish. We've added companies who choose to send birthday and/or work anniversary gifts to employees and/or customers throughout the year. They give us a list – we manage everything from there. It is something we've nurtured and grown. (If you know anyone interested in this service – you can send them here to learn more).

While this is clearly not 'pruning' for these companies, it is something they do as part of a long term view. They are nurturing relationships with the people who are critical to their business. While I'm sure they get positive feedback from some of the customers and employees about the cookies and brownies, the benefits are real but may not be immediately evident. A great harvest takes time to develop.

Life has gotten busy in the past few summers and I must admit that I have not had the chance to check on the blueberry bushes as often as I should. Last week I had the opportunity to make a trip down to the camp for a little R&R. When I walked out to the garden area to check on the blueberry bushes, it was overwhelming.

In the nearly 30 years I've been going down there, I remember harvesting blueberries, but not like this. I spent several hours over two afternoons picking nearly three gallons of these beautiful berries, marveling at the bounty the bushes offered up. And I am certain that the crystal blue Carolina sky, cool breezes off the creek and the summer rains will produce even more of this bounty throughout the rest of the season.

Would any of these things happened if I had not chosen to prune and clean? To make tough decisions? To do the hard work without immediate payback? Probably not.

We hope that when our customers send a gift from Anna's Gourmet Goodies, they'll get immediate feedback at least some of the time. Then again, they might not. I do, however, believe that when you take the longer view, somewhere down the road the harvest comes in. And if it's anything like the yield from the blueberry bushes, you might need a bigger bowl.

Do your homework

Original Post Date: October 9, 2009

I remember the first time someone said this to me at work. It felt like I was being jabbed with a needle. Not that it was unwarranted, he was right. I was expressing my opinion on a technology solution which was simply that - my opinion. It was not however, rooted in the facts. I had not done my homework. It was a lesson I still remember and practice to this day.

Someday, I hope that Anna will thank me. It'll probably take her a while to understand, but the lessons and lectures on homework and discipline I seem to dole out on a regular basis will pay off for her in the future. Like any athlete that expects to reach the top of their sport, discipline and practice are not optional. Schoolwork and academics are no different.

I'm certainly not perfect in this area, but I have learned the value of research and preparation over the years. When I was working in the technology world, one of my associates used to always say, "It's not enough to know the answer, you have to understand why". I believe that you can apply this principle to many areas of business and life. Certainly it plays a role in baking our gourmet cookies, and I practice this philosophy in the business side of Anna's Gourmet Goodies as well.

Baking is really about science and chemistry. Ultimately, you are trying to take moisture out of natural materials at a rate that allows all the ingredients to blend together just perfectly. I can throw together a sauté dish of veggies and meat for dinner with my eyes closed, but making a batch of 10,000 cookies where each one will come out precisely the same, requires research, diligence and doing your homework. Whether or not Anna will ever step behind the mixer and fire up the oven is yet to be seen, but I am still going to insist that she develop the muscle required to approach problems and opportunities logically, and do her research.

We apply the same principle to conducting business with our clients. It is not uncommon for us to receive an order with what appears to be an error in the shipping address. We could simply ship the product as ordered and let the chips fall where they may. Instead, we choose to do some basic research on the Internet first, before contacting the customer for clarification. Sure, it takes a little extra time to do this work, but in the end, it is one of the features of our service that differentiates us in the marketplace.

I do the same when contacting new prospects or vendors. Before I ever pick up the phone, I'll do my homework to make sure that I have a basic understanding of the business I am calling. How easy was it to find them on the Internet? Is their website up to date with contact info? What about products and services – is it easy to find out what they do or sell? Is the owner or management team listed?

It is a habit I've developed that truly pays dividends when it comes to building long term relationships with clients. It helps us build our customer base, as well as selecting our suppliers, because we expect the same level of service and commitment from those companies that support our business, that we provide to our clients. Ultimately, we attract and retain customers and suppliers that are truly a pleasure to do business with. Life's too short to have it any other way.

So if you and your company decide to send gifts from Anna's Gourmet Goodies, you can rest assured that we'll take some time to do our homework on your business. If there is something we can do to help, even if it has nothing to do with cookies, I'm happy to share our experience. And, if you are a supplier looking to work with Anna's Gourmet Goodies, I'd recommend you at least visit our website and do a little research before you make that first call. If you think it's not that important, just ask Anna how Dad feels about doing your homework.

Don't Look Back

Original Post Date: March 11, 2009

Odds are you've probably heard the phrase, 'hindsight is 20/20'. It means that when we look back at life or a business, it's always easy to see clearly what we should or should not have done. But when you are in the arena, you simply can't do that. Race car drivers know this all too well. Spending more than a few milliseconds looking in the rear view mirror can spell disaster.

We've not had much snow lately in North Carolina, but last week we did see a pretty good dusting. Enough to allow me to take Anna over to the park for a short ride down the hill on a sledding tub. I don't get on a sled much anymore, and while I enjoyed the ride, it did bring back a vivid memory and a lesson from my younger days.

Now that my parents have both passed on to the next life, I can safely tell this story. Although I expect my mom knew what happened all along, as only mothers can. It was a painful life lesson about looking backwards when you should be focused on where you are going.

We did not have continuous snow cover in Kentucky, but when the ground was white, I was probably outside on a sled. One snowy afternoon when I was 15, my friend Wayne (who already had his driver's license) and I planned a trip to George Rogers Clark Park for a little sledding. We picked up his girlfriend at the time and headed out to the park, bundled up and ready for some fast downhill action.

We met some folks at the park that were riding downhill on a car hood. Seemed like a cool idea at the time. It was wide and fast and totally out of control; the perfect draw for a couple of teenagers out for an afternoon of adventure.

I do remember thinking that my mom would most certainly not approve of me riding down the hill on the hood of a car. Partly because it was not safe with all the metal edges and mostly because she knew better – I did not. But the parents were not around, we were on an adventure and I hopped on for the ride.

The three of us started off down the hill all facing in the right direction. Yes, it was fast and it was fun. Not too far into the ride, we hit a bump, tossing my other two passengers off and spinning me around so I continued down the hill backwards. I was looking back up at Wayne and remember him waving, laughing and yelling. I turned around to look where I was going and a split second later, I made contact with the tree.

It stopped me completely. Fortunately, I was wearing several layers of clothing and luckily I impacted the tree about two inches to the right of my spine, dead center in the largest muscle of my back. My head snapped back, but missed the tree. Had I landed a few inches the other way with my spine taking the impact, I probably would not have walked away and might not be writing this post as well.

They helped me back up the hill and slid me into the car. It felt like I had cracked something, but I was too scared to go to a doctor. Wayne dropped me off at my house and left quickly before anyone could ask where we had been. I went straight to my room, got in bed, and said my prayers for not ending up in the ER. I never said anything to Mom, but I'm sure she knew something was not quite right.

I try to look back on these life events and see if I can learn something so I don't have to go through that pain a second time. For me, I believe this was an example of the value of looking forward when you are going somewhere fast. Running a business, in today's spiraling economic climate, reminds me of my sledding adventure and the importance of staying focused on where you are heading.

At Anna's Gourmet Goodies, we try to do just that. We've introduced a new line of packaging with bright colors, are adding some new services for our business clients, and continue to look for ways where we can add value to our existing customers as well as new clients. Debbie and I are shaping some ideas for a new website that we hope to launch shortly. We're moving forward fast, watching where we are going and not continually looking backwards.

Don't get me wrong – history is important. You have to know where you've come from to get a clear sense of where you are going. But, there is a time to look back and be reflective, and a time to look forward. When you are racing down a hill or running a business in a fast changing environment like we have today, you'd better stay focused on where you are headed or you just might hit a tree.

Do you sleep in a storm?

Original Post Date: October 23, 2010

Benjamin Franklin said that "If you fail to plan, you are planning to fail". I don't believe that this founding father was telling us to eliminate all spontaneity in our life and work. I believe that what he wanted us to learn was that planning is actually the path to freedom. We are only as free as our options. We'll never be able to account for every eventuality we encounter, but having a plan gives us a guideline on how to react, which is the most important determinate of outcome in life and in business.

There are a number of ad campaigns that have, to the creator's delight, left an indelible mark in my brain. I was watching the Super Bowl when the original Macintosh ad ran – still gives me chills to think about it. I loved the Budweiser ad when the farmers clapped for the Olympic torch runner. And if you're familiar with American Standard Air Conditioning, my friend Mike Minogue from DarkHorse Creative is responsible for the 'Maybe it's too comfortable' series of ads.

But in my mental file cabinet, is one series for the Boy Scouts of America. It featured several famous people, including President Gerald Ford. The theme of the campaign was centered on the concept that you never know where scouting will take you. I was a Boy Scout, and while I can't claim to recite the pledge and probably won't become President, I do remember the motto, 'Be Prepared'; two powerful words that provide a valuable lesson for life and business.

2010 Men's Retreat

I recently attended the 2010 Men's Retreat hosted by August Turak at his farm. A group of very successful entrepreneurs, attorneys, teachers, consultants, a black belt, and others from various walks of life, gathered not for idle chit chat about sports, females, or money, but to explore their faith and share their toughest and most intimate personal and business challenges. To understand what it means to 'spend time in the desert' as Joseph Campbell describes in his book, "The Hero's Journey". And, ultimately, to prepare for the challenges we will all face in our lives.

The study materials for the weekend came from the Bible and were based on The Book of Job. An article entitled, 'The Cup of Trembling' provided the basis for discussions among the group. Perhaps it was the stunning scenery, the abundant and wonderful food, or simply Augie's hospitality, but I cannot recall spending time with a group of men so engaged and open about their triumphs, their tragedies, and the challenges that lay ahead.

Each one of us has faced, or will face, tragedy and setbacks in our life, our family, and in business. Augie once told me that, "A small business owner dies a thousand deaths". I understand completely. Baking cookies is honestly a pretty good occupation, but running and managing a business with world class service, like Anna's Gourmet Goodies is tough and there are ups and downs like waves in the ocean. The key to surviving and succeeding is to understand and accept that adversity and 'time in the desert' is a part of the process. You can embrace it and gain strength to persevere, or wallow around and ultimately die of thirst – it is your choice.

One of the readings from the weekend was an excerpt from Mitch Albom's book, 'have a little faith' – taken from one of 'The Reb's' sermons. In it, he describes a farm hand looking for a job. The man presents his letter of recommendation from his former employer that states simply, "He sleeps in a storm".

After he is hired, a terrible storm comes up and the owner panics, calling for the hired hand to help secure the farm. But he does not answer. When the owner runs out into the storm to check the animals, the hay and the grain, he finds that all are secure, in preparation for the storm. The hired hand is sleeping.

Storms will come. Again and again. The question that I ask myself, and you might as well, is this; are you prepared? People ask me about Anna's Gourmet Goodies all the time, and I'd be untruthful if I said that we have not weathered our fair share of storms over the past 9 years or so. And in my personal life, I've spent some time in the desert as well. But through it all, we try very hard to take care of our resources, to cover the hay and lock up the grain, so that we can sleep through the storm.

As I was editing the video for this blog post just after midnight, something happened to my computer that I cannot explain. All of the icons from my desktop disappeared and some of the files that I had saved were gone. But every day, I create a complete image of my machine. So I simply backed up the current files, started the restore process, and went to sleep, knowing that when I woke up, the sun would be out and my computer would be running again with everything in place, ready for the next storm.

Doing the real work

Original Post Date: January 22, 2012

There is a movement afoot by consumers to understand where our food really comes from. Instead of simply walking into a store, filling up a basket, and stuffing the items in the pantry and the fridge, people are again getting curious about who is actually producing what we eat. That's a good thing. The farmers and crafts people who do the work of producing and preparing our food is not a growing population and understanding the work they do is vitally important to our culture and our future.

I love to drive out into the country and visit our suppliers. It is one of my favorite things to do at Anna's Gourmet Goodies. While we don't visit with everyone who makes products for our cookies, there is something special about getting to know the people who work so hard to make the ingredients we use. They are doing the work that most folks probably think little about on a day to day basis. Cathy, June, Dewey, Terry, Frank, Ray, and many others go about their daily task to bring the staples of life to our table. They are doing the real work.

As we always like to do just before Christmas, Anna and I headed out on our day trip together, visiting, sharing and thanking those people who helped our business during the year. This past December, we decided to visit the suppliers for our Artisan Cookies, Lindley Mills, Latta's Egg Ranch, and Homeland Creamery.

Our first stop was at Lindley Mills. I've been buying flour direct from the mill since about 2003. I cannot remember ever walking in the door and seeing anything other than a beaming smile from June and Cathy (even when I don't have cookies in hand). They don't check email on their phones or hide behind some terminal (they don't have Internet access at the mill). They always have time for catching up and asking about our business.

While we are there picking up our comparatively small order, they'll be loading semi-tractor trailers with product bound for large bakeries and distributors. Everyone will be greeted with the same warmth and genuine caring. Dewey gets off the forklift, throws a couple of 25 pound sacks on his shoulders, and carefully loads up our vehicle by hand. As always, he smiles and wishes me a nice afternoon.

I've had the opportunity to sit and visit with Joe Lindley and I understand exactly why the people at Lindley Mills are like they are. His philosophy of building sincere, long term relationships with his customers is not some business strategy, it is simply who they are and how they live. He works hard to build and run his business so that the business can take care of the people who work hard for him.

Our next stop was the Homeland Creamery in Julian, NC. Terri was still out to lunch so we visited with Cookie (that's her name, seriously – imagine that). She works at the retail operation, along with her 'adopted' sister and her sister's daughter. Practically everyone who works there comes from the local community or their church. The Bowman Family that runs the dairy is a sixth (heading into seventh) generation of farmers caring for the animals and the land. This is truly a community and family business.

Talking with them, you get a sense that working at the Creamery is not simply another job, but a way of life that you probably won't find in corporate retail operations. It's a mild day in December with just a touch of rain falling, but there is a steady flow of customers driving miles from the nearest town for a scoop of ice cream. Everyone is served with a smile and leaves with a smile.

Terri came back from lunch and we visited for a while, talking about business and our plans for 2012. It was going on 2:00 p.m. and 'The Girls' were beginning to make their way to the barn, heavy with milk and looking forward to getting a little relief. In a few days, when much of the world is fast asleep looking forward to Christmas morning, 'The Girls' will wander toward the barn around 2:00 a.m. and a group of farm hands will do the work of taking their milk, just as they do every day of the week, 365 days a year.

Our final stop was at Latta's Egg Ranch. When we arrived, Frank Latta had left, but Ray was there just finishing up the afternoon's egg packing. Ray has been working on the farm since he was old enough to walk. I've watched him stand over the light table, carefully inspecting each egg for cracks, embryos or other imperfections before they get packaged.

It is the same routine that happens every day, 365 days a year at Latta's egg ranch. On Christmas morning, they'll be out gathering the eggs before breakfast, just as they do every day because chickens lay eggs every day. And someone has to care for them. Frank, Ray and the rest of the Latta family do just that.

Visiting with our suppliers and getting to know the people that work there, is an incredibly valuable part of our business. They are doing real work, every single day that adds value to our business and touches the lives of many people. Not just in our local area, but around the country.

At Anna's Gourmet Goodies, our customers place orders on our website, over the phone and by email. We have never met or spoken to many of our customers. But I want you to know that despite using technology to facilitate the transaction part of our business, we understand and value those people who 'do the work'. We try to connect with them. And we put that same effort and passion into the cookies we make. Each one by hand – weighed before it is baked. Packed with love and care, and sent off to someone, somewhere, with the hope that when they take that first bite, they'll feel that connection back to those who are doing the work, every day of the year, to put food on our table.

On changes, the elephant, the rider and the path forward

Original Post Date: June 29, 2016

Do you embrace change? Seek it out? You might, but the majority of people tend to resist change in at least some area of life or work. The truth is that like most things, it requires balance. Too much, and nothing gets done. Not enough and you never move forward. Like most problems to be solved, the first steps are observation and learning.

Mark Twain said, "The only person who likes a change, is a wet baby". Do you like change? The truth is, it really doesn't matter whether you like it or not, change comes in life and in business. We've experienced a few milestones recently that mark change at Anna's Gourmet Goodies and in the Duke household.

I shared the story recently of how we started our business selling pies and cheesecakes. Like many startups, we did everything by hand until purchasing equipment to help us scale the business and keep up with demand. A dough roller quickly turned those rounds of dough into perfectly formed pie crusts, before carefully placing them in the pans by hand. A cake cutter from Food Tools helped us pre-slice pies and cheesecakes, inserting a sheet of parchment paper between the slices (you've probably seen this before in some warehouse clubs.

We sold both pieces of equipment and shipped them off to their new owners, a baker in Minnesota and a restaurant in Arizona. While it was nice to pocket cash for equipment we haven't used in years, it was a bittersweet moment to see it leave the bakery. We spent a lot of hours together.

In our personal life we're also facing changes, getting ready to ship off our most prized possession and the company namesake off to college. Anna graduated from high school and is preparing for the next leg of her journey in just a few short weeks. The decision to leave SciQuest and start Anna's Gourmet Goodies was complex and based in no small part on my desire to spend as much time as possible with my little girl, now a young woman. Change happens.

A few years ago I was fortunate enough to meet Dan Heath, one of the authors of "Switch: How to Change when Change is Hard". He was concluding his book tour at Duke's Fuqua School of Business and I decided to take Anna along. She was just about to head into the teenage years, our business was undergoing some transition, and learning about change from an expert seemed to be perfect timing.

We sat in the front row. The audience was a mix of MBA students, alumni and business executives. I'm pretty confident that Anna was in fact, the youngest person in the room. When Dan came out on stage, he immediately noticed her and his facial expression confirmed that the age range of his audience would begin a little younger than he expected. Years later after the release of his next book "Decisive", we chatted and laughed about that moment.

The Heath brothers present a framework for understanding change that I still think about to this day. It is simple, profound and makes more sense to me than programs based on lists, goals, exercises or whatever. It is based on the concept of an elephant, a rider and a path.

The elephant represents our emotional self. It is large, sometimes unwieldy and can be difficult to turn on a dime and move in another direction.

The rider represents our logical self. The rider can quickly assess a situation, apply lessons learned and come up with a decision on the best direction to proceed. Sounds easy, right?

Here's the problem, the elephant does not always agree with the rider. And while the rider likes to think he's in control, moving an elephant can be hard. What's the answer? Find a path that works for both the elephant and the rider.

If you've ever raised a teenager or know someone who has, the elephant and the rider analogy probably rings true. Think of the teenager as the elephant, you are the rider and you're looking for that path.

As parents we've worked diligently to keep Anna on a path that will allow her to achieve her potential. That's about as much as any parent can hope for.

As for Anna's Gourmet Goodies, we've also been moving along a path that we hope leads us to a place where we can continue to grow our potential. It was hard giving up the wholesale dessert business to focus strictly on cookie and brownie gifts. Along the way, the elephant veered off into a few brier patches (yes, those thorns are painful).

But we've always tried to stay true to the values that led us to found the company. Not because it looks good on a piece of paper, but rather because we know that ultimately, the best way to deal with changes every business faces, is to keep the elephant and the rider on a path where they are both comfortable.

One of the benefits of that mindset comes when we make a connection with our customer's elephant and rider. When we provide a path for them that makes sense for their marketing, employee satisfaction, or branding goals by sending out our gourmet cookie gifts, it really is magical.

If you are facing change in your personal or business life, and it seems hard, stop beating yourself up. Pick up a copy of Switch and spend some time getting to know the elephant and the rider. Of course, you could also order a box of chocolate chip cookies, get yourself a tall, cold glass of milk and sit out on the porch to contemplate your path.

While I can't speak for your elephant and rider, I can say that mine are always happy to go down that path.

More Information

Here is information on the businesses, websites and other references from the posts.

Homeland Creamery
6506 Bowman Dairy Rd
Julian, NC 27283
http://www.homelandcreamery.com/

Paddle Creek Outfitters
https://paddlecreeknc.com/

Kayak Paddling Basics
https://www.thoughtco.com/reasons-kayaks-are-better-than-canoes-2555697

Paddling.com
https://paddling.com/

The Secrets of Jesuit Breadmaking
https://www.amazon.com/Secrets-Jesuit-Breadmaking-Rick-Curry/dp/0060951184/
https://www.barnesandnoble.com/w/secrets-of-jesuit-breadmaking-rick-curry/1000297582

Articles on Brother Curry
http://www.nytimes.com/1994/03/23/garden/bread-as-food-for-body-and-soul.html
http://americamagazine.org/content/all-things/remembering-jesuit-father-rick-curry
http://www.georgetowner.com/articles/2015/dec/21/father-rick-curry-sj-co-founder-dog-tag-bakery-has-died/

Brother Curry on 60 Minutes
https://youtu.be/29sF1iYyYSY

Haw River Canoe and Kayak Company
http://hawrivercanoe.com/

Saxapahaw General Store
http://saxgenstore.com/

Kentucky Bourbon
https://en.wikipedia.org/wiki/Bourbon_whiskey

Jeff Slater
The Marketing Sage
http://www.themarketingsage.com/

Fanny Slater - cookbook author and TV personality
http://www.fannyslater.com/
http://www.amazon.com/Orange-Lavender-Figs-Fanny-Slater/dp/1476796300/

Alan Hoffler
Millwyck Communications
http://www.millswyck.com/

Crossroads Infiniti
http://www.crossroadsinfiniti.com/

One Word that will change your life
http://www.amazon.com/Word-That-Will-Change-Expanded/dp/1118809424/

NC Workhorse and Mule Association
c/o Debbie Denton
10501 Ramsey Street
Linden, NC 28356
910-980-0125

David's Noodle Bar
http://www.ddandnb.com/

Best Burgers in North Carolina
http://www.onlyinyourstate.com/north-carolina/burgers-in-nc/

Johnson's Drive In - Our State Magazine
https://www.ourstate.com/johnsons-drive-in/

Malcolm Gladwell - The Outliers
http://gladwell.com/outliers/the-10000-hour-rule/

The Internet Summit
http://internetsummit.com/

Sisarina - a Brand Strategy Agency
https://sisarina.com/

Scissor Artists
Karl Johnson
http://www.cutarts.com/
Erik Johnson
https://www.facebook.com/eriksilhouettes/

The Big Shopping Cart
http://www.gottobenc.com/promotions/big-cart

Dan Dye - silversmith
http://www.dandye.com/

Chris Brogan - author, journalist, marketing consultant
http://owner.media/

LaFarm Bakery
https://www.lafarmbakery.com/

Back Alley Coffee Roasters
http://www.backalleyroasters.com/

Jim Karrh - Consultant
http://www.jimkarrh.com/

Annalise's Friends
http://annalisesfriends.org/

The Shepherd's Table Soup Kitchen
http://www.shepherds-table.org/

Simon Sinek's Ted Talk on 'The Why'
https://www.ted.com/talks/simon_sinek_how_great_leaders
_inspire_action

Durward Matheny, Forensic Document Examiner
http://durwardmatheny.com/

Koinonia Foundation
http://www.koinoniawf.org/

Duke Cancer Center of Raleigh
https://www.dukehealth.org/locations/duke-cancer-center-
raleigh

1in9 Foundation
http://www.1in9.com/

Ronald McDonald House of Durham
http://www.rmhdurhamwake.org/

Wake Forest Civitan Club
http://civitan.net/wakeforest/

The Backyard Bistro
http://www.backyardbistro.com/

Darkhorse Design
http://www.darkhorsewins.com/

August Turak - author, speaker, teacher
http://www.augustturak.com/

Have a Little Faith: A True Story by Mitch Albom
http://www.amazon.com/Have-Little-Faith-True-Story/dp/0786868724/

Lindley Mills
http://www.lindleymills.com/

Chip and Dan Heath
http://heathbrothers.com/about/

Their book - Switch: How to Change Things When Change Is Hard
http://heathbrothers.com/books/switch/

Your notes

www.ingramcontent.com/pod-product-compliance
Lightning Source LLC
Chambersburg PA
CBHW051310220526
45468CB00004B/1287